Schoch

LADIES OF
LEGACY

AMBER ALBEE SWENSON

WESTBOW
PRESS®
A DIVISION OF THOMAS NELSON
& ZONDERVAN

Unless stated otherwise, all Scripture quotations are from the New International Version.

WestBow Press books may be ordered through booksellers or by contacting:

WestBow Press
A Division of Thomas Nelson & Zondervan
1663 Liberty Drive
Bloomington, IN 47403
www.westbowpress.com
1 (866) 928-1240

ISBN: 978-1-5127-2951-1 (sc)
ISBN: 978-1-5127-2952-8 (hc)
ISBN: 978-1-5127-2950-4 (e)

Library of Congress Control Number: 2016901726

Print information available on the last page.

WestBow Press rev. date: 02/24/2016

In memory of all the ladies who carried the torch of the gospel.

I thank God for your passion and perseverance.

Thank You, Lord, for the truth and transparency of their lives.

Lesson One

Miriam

Read Exodus 2:1–8; 15:19–21; and Numbers 12.

Devotion: In the earliest account of Miriam, we see her as a girl sent to watch her brother, Moses, who was floating in a basket on the water. We aren't told her age at that time, but we see that from her youth, Miriam was given a great deal of responsibility. Just as the Lord's hand was on Moses to prepare him for leadership, God guided and shaped Miriam as well.

In Exodus 15, Miriam was a great leader. The Israelites had just left Egypt, where they witnessed the Passover, which spared their children, while the Egyptians' firstborn were killed. The Israelites were hunted down and faced certain death until God miraculously parted the Red Sea. When the sea returned to its former position, and the Egyptian men pursing the Israelites drowned, Miriam's first impulse was to worship and praise God for saving them. How pleasing to the Lord to set such an example!

Miriam teaches us to give thanks and praise to God in all situations, even if we are on the side of a sea with nothing but desert ahead. We can always find something that doesn't fit our expectations. It's better to be grateful for the blessings in our lives rather than disgruntled over the irritants.

The events of Numbers 12 do not paint Miriam in such an attractive light. We aren't told anything about Moses' Cushite wife, but something caused Miriam and Aaron to rebel against Moses and the leadership position God had given him.

"'Has the Lord spoken only through Moses?' they asked. 'Hasn't He also spoken through us?'" (Num. 12:2). These words drip with arrogance. Miriam and Aaron were haughty about the fact that God had spoken through them. This attitude is in stark contrast to Moses' spirit. In Numbers 11 Moses said, "I wish that all the Lord's people were prophets and that the Lord would put His Spirit on them" (v. 29). He didn't lord over anyone that God had called him up the mountain and had spoken directly to him. Moses' desire was that everyone would walk with God as he had. He wished everyone would enjoy the fellowship of God, and in turn respond with obedience.

What a difference there would have been in the Old Testament if that had been the case. Instead of complaining and showing disbelief, the Israelites would have remained faithful, trusting in God who had rescued them so many times. If the people had been in the Spirit, they would have replaced their grumbling with contentment and joy, peace and patience.

What a difference we would see in our Christian community today if we had that same selfless attitude. So often we want *our* church, *our* mission, *our* ministry to flourish. It would be better to pray for hearts to be changed and souls to be saved, regardless of who delivers the message.

The apostle Paul expressed this sentiment in Philippians 1:15-18. "It is true that some preach Christ out of envy and rivalry, but others out of goodwill. The latter do so out of love, knowing that I am put here for the defense of the gospel. The former preach Christ out of selfish ambition, not sincerely, supposing that they can stir up trouble for me while I am in chains. But what does it matter? The important thing is that in every way, whether from false motives or true, Christ is preached. And because of this I rejoice."

We need to become more like Moses and Paul, praying for results. When we've tried to reach someone, we ought to pray God would bring that person to faith, whether through our efforts or someone else's.

And when we see a leader seemingly going in the wrong direction or making bad choices, instead of shaking our heads and throwing up our hands—or worse, gossiping about it—why not commit that leader to God, begging that he or she would get on the right path so God might work mightily through him or her?

Miriam's rebellion against Moses was a grasp at power and an attempt to replace Moses as the leader of Israel. She wasn't content to lead in the capacity she had been given; nor did she acknowledge the divine appointment of Moses.

Oh, can I relate to Miriam. God's Word makes it clear that we are to be subordinate to those God put in authority over us, and yet, my sinful nature often is unwilling to let my husband lead. Haven't we all questioned, mocked or insulted those who govern? Instead of giving leaders respect, understanding that God is the One who put that person above us, it's all too easy to thumb our nose at them, grumble and disobey.

God gave Miriam a leading role. People knew who she was. She had power and prestige and if that wasn't enough, she might have prayed for God to open doors so she could serve more. Instead, Miriam sought advancement by dethroning Moses of his position.

My study Bible notes that since Miriam, and not Aaron, was struck with leprosy, likely Miriam was the instigator of the opposition.[1] That Moses prayed on Miriam's behalf shows the goodness of heart the Lord saw and defended. Moses proved himself time and again to be faithful to God's will. Because of this, when Miriam and Aaron spoke against him, the Lord was swift and severe in His defense of Moses and His chastisement of Miriam.

If we are willing to be content with our lot in life, not only will we be at peace in our own regard, but the Lord will also be pleased with us. Satan seduces us to seek power. That is God's to give, and He gave it to Moses, a "humble man" (Num. 12:3). It is in humility that we lower ourselves to a position where we readily do God's will, not our own.

---

[1] *Concordia Self-Study Bible,* New International Version (St. Louis, MO: Concordia, 1986), 207.

Devotion Question: Is there an authority figure in your life (boss, public official, or pastor) you disdain? Perhaps the person has made sinful choices, and you've experienced the consequences. Maybe he or she has hurt you with words or actions. Maybe you feel he or she is inadequate and that you could do the job better.

The apostle Paul told us to pray for those in authority (1 Tim. 2:1–2). Especially when we don't agree with what they are doing, it's imperative that we bring them before the throne of God. Doing so may result in blessings for us as God changes their hearts and maybe words and actions while giving us the peace of placing the situation in His capable hands. Isn't that a better alternative to quarreling or living with resentment in our hearts?

On the other hand, if God gives you a position of authority, take it seriously and humbly serve where He puts you.

Topics for further study:

USING OUR MOUTHS IN A GOD-PLEASING WAY

1. Read the following passages. Compare and contrast an evil tongue with a righteous tongue.

   Proverbs 11:13

   Proverbs 16:23–24

   Proverbs 16:28

Proverbs 17:27–28

Proverbs 26:20

In James 3, James compared the tongue to a bit in a horse's mouth or the rudder on a ship. The tongue is such a small part of the body, but it has the ability to control our paths.

We can use our tongues to instruct and heal, to encourage and praise, or we can use them to tear down, to deceive and spread gossip. How we use them will impact everyone around us.

The person controlled by the sinful nature will hear "dirt" on someone and run home to call or e-mail his or her friends. Such news will sadden the godly woman. She will seek the Lord to resolve the matter, and when and if she is given the opportunity, she will encourage those involved to live biblically. The wise woman will ponder many things in her heart while keeping most of those things from ever leaving her lips.

2. Read the following passages. How can we keep our mouths from sinning?

    Psalm 17:3

    Psalm 141:3

    1 Timothy 5:13-14

These passages give us a pretty good course of action. First, resolve not to sin by gossiping, exaggerating, complaining, cursing, or humiliating with your mouth. Second, pray for help. Third, keep yourself busy by serving the Lord and others. Instead of reaching for the phone or getting on the computer to talk about someone or complain about something, take time to sit with your Bible, pray, or scrub the bathroom while asking the Lord to intervene.

Finally, find a godly woman to go to when you need to talk about the issues in your life, someone who will remind you of the Lord's promises, instruct you in God's ways, and remind you to go to the Lord in prayer and Bible study.

BEING IN THE HANDS OF THE LORD

3. Read Hebrews 10:26–31. First, note that this section is written to believers, not unbelievers who have never come to know the truth of salvation. Verse 26 talks about those who have received the knowledge of the truth. Verse 30 says God will judge His people. What word in verse 31 describes what it's like to "fall into the hands of the living God"?

4. Look again at verse 26. What type of sin evokes falling into the hands of the living God?

5. To paraphrase, verse 29 says deliberately sinning _against_ the Son of God, treats Christ's blood (the sacrifice) as _unholy_ and _insults_ the Spirit.

Those are strong words; words we should take to heart.

6. Read 2 Samuel 11:1–15, 26–27; and 12:13–23. What did David do that resulted in his falling into the hands of the living God?

7. Was his sin deliberate? How do you know (11:3)?

8. Why did Nathan say the child would die (12:14)?

9. *Contempt* is "the feeling one has toward somebody or something one considers low, worthless, etc." [2] Nathan told David that David's sin showed "utter contempt" or complete and total disrespect. Willful disobedience is like spitting in a person's face. Think of how many times you've thought or even said, "I shouldn't, but …" Whether it's grabbing an extra piece of dessert after you've stuffed yourself, talking about someone in ways you shouldn't, or spending money you don't have on clothes, furniture, or a handbag you don't need, we all succumb to willful disobedience from time to time. Nathan shows us that sometimes, even often, others suffer from our willful disobedience. Gossiping hurts another person's feelings and maybe his or her reputation. Depending on who you gossip to, it may hurt your reputation. Routine overindulging may impact those around you as your fatigue and weight leave you unable to do tasks.

---

[2] Noah Webster, Webster's New World Dictionary, 3rd College ed. (New York: Berkley Books, 1984), s.v. "contempt."

What is your weakness when it comes to willful disobedience, and what are you going to do to combat it?

10. Read Jonah 1:1–17. What did Jonah do to fall into the hands of the living God?

11. Were his actions deliberate? How do you know (1:10)?

12. David did what he knew was wrong. Jonah refused to do what he knew was right. This mistake is equally easy for us to do. Have you ever spent your day off work sitting in front of the TV or computer instead of being productive? Have you deliberately missed the call from your pastor or another person at church because you were pretty sure he or she wanted you to do something? Have you made excuses, maybe even lied, so you didn't have to do something?

13. Read the following passages. It's easy to forget that our money, talent, health, or strength isn't just for us. How do these passages force us to think differently about those things?

Luke 12:48b

Ephesians 2:10

1 Peter 4:10

14. Read Acts 9:1–19. What did Saul do to end up in the hands of the living God?

Not only was Saul deliberate in his persecution of Christians, but he thought his actions were pleasing to God.

15. Have you ever gotten into an argument on Facebook, thinking you were doing so for God's glory, when really you were wasting your time and delivering a tone that wasn't doing anything to bring Him glory? I have! In fact, on one occasion a godly friend warned me about getting involved, knowing it wouldn't do anything to change minds and that I would likely get devoured, but I went in anyway. What other deeds do we do, thinking we're doing them for God or bringing Him glory, when really we're not?

16. When did these men's time "in the hands of the living God" end?

17. What can we learn from this?

In some circles we like to make a distinction between punishment and chastisement. God punished Jesus for our sins, so we don't receive a punishment from God, only a chastisement. The word *chastise* means "to punish.[3]" It's important to note that we cannot pay for our sins. Only Christ could do that with His perfect

---

[3] Webster's New World Dictionary, 3rd College ed., s.v. "chastise."

life and death. When the Lord chastises us, He does so with the intention of turning us from our sins.

BEING AMBITIOUS VS. Having Ambition

18. Read Matthew 6:24; 20:25–28. What does Jesus say about the world's sense of ambition?

19. Read James 3:14–16. Where does the world's sense of ambition and accomplishment come from?

20. What does James say accompanies selfish ambition?

21. Read Colossians 3:23–24 and 1 Peter 4:10–11. Should Christians be ambitious?

Jesus wants us to dismiss the world's sense of ambition, and James reminds us that this comes from the Devil and is accompanied by envy, disorder, and other evil practices (like stepping on top of others to get ahead). You cannot serve God and money or God and power. Christian leaders have a responsibility to serve but not grasp for power. God may indeed put you in a position of leadership. He may give you authority but not so you can be a dictator and have people serving you while you relax at the expense of others. Those in leadership are given a trust and must work harder than anyone else to keep those beneath them honoring God and working toward godly goals.

When we serve, we ought to serve wholeheartedly and with all our strength. We work hard because we know we work for the Lord to further His kingdom, not our own.

SOMETHING TO THINK ABOUT

Jesus said, "The mouth speaks what the heart is full of" (Matt. 12:34). In other words, the way we talk shows the condition of our hearts. If we are prone to grumbling, likely we are discontent or feel we deserve a better life or more honor than we have been given.

The Bible tells us exactly what we deserve. "The wages of sin is death" (Rom. 6:23).

Consider Joseph. When he was sold into slavery, he worked hard for Potiphar, even though this wasn't where he wanted to be. When he was put in prison, he again showed he was able to lead, even if he was at the bottom. How we react when things are less than ideal shows God whether we truly are dedicated to serving Him or if we seek an easy life for ourselves, regardless of God's plan for our lives.

Prayer to close the lesson:

Dear heavenly Father, surely You are too pure to look down on us and see our shortcomings. Forgive us for the way we have used our mouths to belittle those You have placed in authority above us and those You have placed in our lives to help. We pray with David that You would set a guard over our mouths. Stop sinful talk from leaving our lips. Instead, let our lips be instruments of encouragement, healing, and praise. Keep us from falling into sin. Keep Satan from establishing footholds in our lives that would keep us from serving You. Let our only ambition in life be to serve You and bring glory and honor to Your name. In our Savior's name we pray. Amen.

Lesson Two

Rahab

Read Joshua 2, 6:22–25.

Devotion: The first fact the Bible tells us about Rahab is that she was a prostitute. Though my Bible footnotes the possibility that she was "just" an innkeeper, Scripture again refers to her as a prostitute in Joshua 6; Hebrews 11:31; and James 2:25. From this data we can ascertain that at some point she earned her living as a woman of ill repute.

The second fact we learn about Rahab is that she lied not only to the guards of Jericho but also to the king himself. She not only lied about the men being there but also sent the guards in the wrong direction, allowing the Israelite spies adequate time to get away.

How is it that a lying prostitute found her way into Scripture that speaks about the righteous (Heb. 11:31)?

It wasn't her life of good works that made Rahab righteous before God but rather her faith that the God of Israel was the true God. She'd heard about the Red Sea's parting and the way the

Israelites had conquered the Amorites, and she believed these events could have happened only because the Israelites walked with the one true God.

Rahab's actions with the spies were a consequence of her belief that they were ambassadors of a King greater than the king of Jericho. She further showed this belief by following the spies' instructions flawlessly. She brought her family to her house and hung the scarlet cord from the window in faith. She believed that, just as the water had turned to dry land and so rescued the people of Israel from Pharaoh, if she stepped out in faith, her family would be spared the destruction of Jericho.

Scripture doesn't tell us, but I wonder whether there wasn't grumbling among some of the Israelite women when Rahab and her family were brought to the outskirts of the camp. I've been one to remark about what someone wore to church and tsk-tsked to hear the less-than-proper language another member used. I've mentally gasped to see the Christian leader acting in a less than becoming manner. Such reactions allude to the fact that I feel "those people" are somehow beneath me, maybe even questioning whether "those people" belong in God's house, especially in leadership.

Anytime I think that way, I am the one who doesn't measure up before God. Man looks and cares about the outward appearance, but the Lord looks at the heart (1 Sam. 16:7). Jesus made it clear that He came for the sinner (Mark 2:17).

Whatever sins Rahab committed in her years before meeting the spies were erased with her words, "For the Lord your God is

God in heaven above and on the earth below" (Josh. 2:11). It would be tragic if we saved the Word of God only for those we felt deserved it. None of us deserve to know God or to be saved, and our worldly standards are misleading. Those who think themselves wise and learned, and those who find comfort in their wealth and wisdom, often reject the good news. Jesus said the shepherd would leave the righteous to seek out the straying (Luke 19:10). He does this so those in every walk of life may come to know Him as their Savior.

When the Jews brought the woman caught in adultery to Jesus on their way to stone her, Jesus showed us that her sin was no worse than ours. With His words, "If anyone of you is without sin, let him be the first to throw a stone at her" (John 8:7), we are assured before God that all sin is rebellion. Jesus said that anyone who looks at another person lustfully has already committed adultery with that person in his or her heart (Matt. 5:28). With that as our standard, we must confess that we have all committed adultery.

Remember, too, that Jesus stayed back by the well in Samaria, knowing He would meet the woman who had five husbands and was living with a man out of wedlock. It is so easy for us to point a finger and accuse "that man" or "that woman." Satan is the real Enemy, the one who tempts "that man," "that woman," and us.

Thankfully Jesus came to save sinners. Even as He was dying, Jesus took time to talk with the sinner next to Him on the cross. Thankfully Jesus reaches for us when we stray, too. When He carries us back, His love and mercy are our motivation to show love and mercy to others.

By God's strength we can meet others' sins and weaknesses with compassion and empathy instead of upturned noses. The man or woman who struggles to shake his or her smoking habit is no worse than the man or woman who struggles with his or her weight, exaggeration, sexual immorality, or pride.

"All of us have become like one who is unclean, and all our righteous acts are like filthy rags; we all shrivel up like a leaf, and like the wind our sins sweep us away" (Isa. 64:6).

Devotion Question: Whom do you look down on? We all have someone who has rubbed us the wrong way, either by his or her thoughtless words and actions or by a tendency that drives us crazy.

Here are two tips that may help us quit thinking of that person as less valuable than we are: (1) Put that person at the top of your prayer list and determine to pray for him or her every day, especially for his or her spiritual growth. (2) When you see or hear about the person, remind yourself that he or she is a child of God. Even if the person is an unbeliever, he or she is someone God created, and someone God would love to see saved.

Topics for further study:

Faith and Deeds

1. Read Ephesians 2:8–9. How are we saved?

2. How much of our salvation depends on our works?

Believe it or not, this issue can be a stumbling block. Those who have lived in sin for their whole lives can't imagine they are worthy of God's love. And those who by all appearances have it all together might think they've done pretty well and deserve God's grace.

Paul said in Romans 3:20, "Therefore no one will be declared righteous in his sight by observing the law; rather, through the law we become conscious of sin."

If that's the case, why try to be good? If you don't know the answer, read on.

3. Read Ephesians 2:10. Why were we created?

4. When did God decide what good works He'd like us to do?

5. Read Esther 2:7–9, 17. What traits did God give Esther that put her in the position to save God's people?

6. Read Daniel 1:3–4, 6, 17. What traits did God give Daniel and his friends so they might serve the king of Babylon and God's people?

7. Take some time to really examine yourself. What traits has God given you?

8. Read 2 Corinthians 5:14–15. What is our motivation for doing good works?

9. Notice the word *compel*. *Compel* means "to force[4]." Christ's love *forces* us to live not just for ourselves but for God. If we don't feel motivated to help anyone or don't see anyone in our lives we can help, what might be missing?

10. Read James 2:14–19, 25–26. James' statement is pretty strong. He said if there are no deeds, there is no faith. Obviously we can't help everyone, and sometimes we see someone who needs help in a way we can't provide. How can we reconcile James's statement with the fact that we cannot help everyone in every way?

I'm of the opinion that there's never a time when we can't help, because each of us, no matter what gifts, talents, or treasures we've been given, is able to pray. Even children are able to think of people who have needs and pray for them. We absolutely cannot help everyone in every way; nor does God expect that of us. But God puts people in my life for me to help in the ways I can. And He puts people in your life to help in the ways you can. I wasn't necessarily called to help the people in your life in the same capacity that you were called to help them. I may have time to spend with people but not have a lot of money. You may have money to help people but

---

[4] Webster's New World Dictionary, 3rd College ed., s.v. "compel."

not have a lot of time. I may be able to minister to people by writing letters, while you may prefer to call someone. There are so many ways to help others and so many people who need help. Lord, help us not to get so wrapped up in our lives that we forget to minister to others.

11. List some ways you can help others, taking into account your gifts, resources, and season of life.

THE HEART OF GOD TOWARD SINNERS

12. Read John 20:19–28. Thomas not only told the disciples he didn't believe Jesus rose from the dead, but in the same stubborn pessimism, he said, "Unless I see the nail marks in his hands and put my finger where the nails were, and put my hand into his side, I will not believe it" (v. 25). What do we learn about Jesus because of His return to Thomas?

13. Read Ezekiel 34:11-12, 15-16. What kind of effort does God put into the flock?

14. How does God feel about the less-than-perfect sheep of the flock?

15. What application does this have for spiritual leaders when it comes to the child who doesn't behave in Sunday school or the woman no one can please?

This flies in the face of our sinful nature which screams, "Just hang out with people you like and who treat you well. You don't need the hassle of other people's troubles or attitude."

16. Read Matthew 18:12-14. What kind of effort should we put into the difficult person in our lives or the unbelieving friend or relative? How so?

17. Read Mark 2:15–17. Who in these verses would consider themselves righteous?

18. What did they think of Jesus?

19. Why did Jesus spend time with sinners?

20. How much time do you spend with people who don't know Jesus? Why is that something to consider?

RIGHTEOUSNESS

21. Read Hebrews 11:6–7. What is required to attain righteousness (v. 7)?

22. What two things do we believe when we have faith that leads to righteousness (v. 6)?

23. When is the last time you earnestly sought God other than during a time of trial?

24. Read Romans 3:21–24. From verse 21, we see that righteousness isn't attained by doing what?

25. That means that no matter how good you are, no matter how many people you help, no matter how many commandments you keep, your own works or efforts to keep the law will never lead to you attain righteousness. Why not (v. 23)?

26. Until you go through the commandments and actually see how often you break them, you may not realize how short you are falling.

    The first commandment says to put God first in your life. Do you always put Him first? What things sometimes take the number one position in our lives instead of God?

27. The second commandment is about revering God's name. Do you ever find yourself using God's name flippantly? In what ways do you use God's name that cheapens it?

28. The third commandment is about church and God's Word. Do you ever go to church just because it's what you do but find yourself drifting off during the hymns, readings, or sermons?

Do you make reading God's Word a priority in your life, or do you often put it on the back burner?

29. The fourth commandment is about showing respect for authority. Do you ever find yourself making fun of those in authority over you, talking behind their backs, or deliberately deciding to dishonor them?

30. The fifth commandment is about protecting life, but Jesus said that includes hating. Have you ever hated people so much that you wished they were dead? Or have you thought how great your life would be if/when they weren't around?

31. The sixth commandment is about lust. Have you ever looked at someone and let your thoughts linger in places they shouldn't go?

32. The seventh commandment is about stealing. Pens, sodas, papers … It's easy to walk away with something that belongs to someone else. What other common and sometimes small things do we steal? Have you ever stolen (wasted) someone's time?

33. The eighth commandment is about how we talk about others. How do we break this commandment?

LADIES OF LEGACY

34. The ninth and tenth commandments are about wanting what we don't have. Have you found yourself wanting what others have: their talent, children, husband, looks, health, finances, or house? Who hasn't?

35. Since there is no way to attain righteousness by keeping the commandments, how do we attain righteousness (v. 22)?

36. Read Isaiah 64:6. This passage says our righteous acts are like filthy rags before God. In what ways does our sinful nature ruin our righteous acts so they become filthy? To get you started … If we do a righteous act to make others notice us, we do so for our own benefit and to fuel our own pride. In what other ways does our sinful nature ruin our righteousness?

Something to Think About

If we are honest with ourselves and each other, we must admit that often we are like the older brother in the parable of the prodigal son. Someone in our lives doesn't measure up to our expectations. It's important that we love sinners right where they are and, at the same time, dare not compromise the Word of God.

The apostle Paul told us to "speak the truth in love" (Eph. 4:15). That means we hold the line on matters of the law while offering grace and forgiveness to the repentant. Offering grace and forgiveness to the unrepentant is quite a different matter.

25

In the parable of the prodigal son, the father didn't grant the prodigal forgiveness while he was still partaking in a sinful lifestyle. If he had, the prodigal may have embraced his sin and never come to repentance (turning from his sin).

The writer of Hebrews reminds us, "If we deliberately keep on sinning after we have received the knowledge of the truth, no sacrifice for sins is left, but only a fearful expectation of judgment and of raging fire that will consume the enemies of God" (10:26).

Being prideful and considering another's sin as more disgusting than yours are wrong, but so are accepting and embracing sin instead of dealing with it.

Prayer to Close the Lesson:

Lord God, heavenly Father, it is so easy to see how we have fallen short. Too often we have let our greed and pride control our lives, and we have turned our backs on those You have called us to help. Forgive us, Lord. Help us to look at all people with the same compassion You have. Help us to seek the broken, the weak, and the intimidated to give them the same hope You give us. Remind us that it is only because of Your mercy that we are Your children. Keep Your love in the forefront of our minds so we may be compelled to love others. In Jesus's name we pray. Amen.

LESSON THREE

Deborah

READ JUDGES 4–5:3, 31.

Devotion: This account started out tragically enough: "The Israelites once again did evil in the eyes of the Lord" (4:1). God seeks obedient hearts, and because "He disciplines those He loves" (Prov. 3:12; Heb. 12:6), God will do what is needed to get our attention. Even when the Lord allowed the Israelites to be sold to Jabin, it took twenty years of cruel oppression before we hear of them crying to the Lord for help.

It is good that this story is recorded for us. Anyone who has worked with someone who has strayed knows the frustration that results from effort after effort going unheeded. The Israelites knew all the Lord had done for them, from the Passover to the crossing of the Red Sea, the manna that was provided in the desert for forty years, the walls of Jericho falling, and the miraculous way the land of Canaan was given into their hands. The Lord hadn't merely given them the law; He'd given them an incentive to follow His decrees by the numerous miracles He performed to save them time and again. He showed them His love and provision were real, His power worthy of praise. He showed Himself to be alive and active in their lives. Still they fell away and didn't turn back until things were really bad.

How many times have you prayed for those straying, only for God to rescue them and for you to see them carry on in their sinful ways until the next time they need prayer? If I'm honest, some things took years for me to learn, things like holding my tongue and submitting to authority. That doesn't mean I wasn't taught, rebuked, or disciplined. It just means my sinful nature is stubborn, and spiritual growth sometimes takes time.

Notice that when the people cried to the Lord, He was ready to rescue them. It's comforting to know that God is open and ready to restore the repentant.

Ezekiel 33:11 says, "As surely as I live, declares the Sovereign Lord, I take no pleasure in the death of the wicked, but rather that they turn from their ways and live. Turn! Turn from your evil ways! Why will you die, O house of Israel?"

Jesus tells us there is rejoicing in heaven over one sinner who repents (Luke 15:7), and He gave us the picture of the father running to meet the prodigal son while he was still a long way off, throwing his arms around that wayward son, and kissing him, thrilled to have him back (Luke 15:20).

If only we were so quick to be merciful; if only grudges and bitterness were removed from our vocabulary. So often we are that unmerciful servant who remembers the little annoyances of others while enjoying the favor of God's abundant grace covering our sin.

We will never get to a point of deserving God's grace. We are all prodigals, all wayward children, all hopelessly lost apart from the rescuing power of Christ. Once we realize this truth, we can offer others the same quick and complete forgiveness.

At the point God delivered Israel, Deborah was their judge. Deborah was the only woman to judge Israel. We aren't told how she came to be a judge, but God put her in that position to do His will.

When she summoned Barak, Deborah not only told him to go to war but also assured him of victory from the Lord (4:6). It seems that something should be easy to undertake if God ensures success. Unfortunately, it's all too easy to be skeptical like Barak. After all, God tells us His Word won't return empty but will accomplish what He desires and will achieve the purposes for which He sent it (Isa. 55:11), and yet so often we hesitate and pass up opportunities to share God's Word.

Barak's answer to God's command wasn't complete disobedience, but it wasn't willful obedience either. It was stipulated obedience: "If you go with me, I will go" (4:8).

In comparison David, "a man after God's own heart" (1 Sam. 13:14), *volunteered* to fight Goliath because he trusted in God's complete ability to grant him success, even as his brothers and the king tried to talk him out of it.

Deborah trusted God and courageously accompanied Barak in battle, and she gave him and all Israel encouragement as they left to find Sisera.

"Go!" she said. "This is the day the Lord has given Sisera into your hands" (4:14). She did not say, "You are armed and ready for battle. Do what you do best." The Lord told Deborah that *He* would lure Sisera and that *He* would deliver him into the hands of the Israelites. Deborah was careful to keep the word given to her to the letter, giving God the credit for what He promised to do. She listened to the Lord, did what He said, trusted Him to be with her, and then gave God the glory as she praised and thanked Him for what He accomplished.

Reading the song of Deborah is reminiscent of Psalm 115:1: "Not to us, O Lord, not to us, but to Your name be the glory." May we learn from the account of Deborah to rejoice when even the vilest of sinners turns, to trust in our Lord and Savior to deliver us from the evil at hand, and to give the praise and glory to Him when He accomplishes this.

Devotion Question: In addition to revealing God's plan of salvation, God's Word gives us a guide for Christian living. God tells us what pleases Him and what doesn't. He gives us direction for living righteously when we're in our youth, when we're married, when we're raising children, and when we are widows.

Do you have a teachable spirit? When you read God's Word, are you convicted? Do you respond with obedience?

When I was a young wife, I didn't agree with some things my husband did. Often I confronted him in a less-than-respectful way. When he questioned my methods, I responded by saying, "I'll treat you with respect when you earn my respect."

Thankfully God brought me to His Word, and as I studied it, I saw that God tells me to respect my husband without disclaimers. I am to treat him with respect, even when I disagree with him.

Often as I study God's Word, I sense His nudging me to live differently. That doesn't happen unless we study God's Word, meditate on it, and apply it to our lives. It's easy to read the Word and think of all the ways someone else isn't keeping it. Try to avoid that tendency and pray that the Holy Spirit would show you your weaknesses and give you the strength to help you overcome them.

Topics for further study:

COURAGE

1. Read 2 Chronicles 19:4–11. Jehoshaphat wasn't talking about the courage of going to war. What kind of courage did he refer to that the judges would need?

2. Why does it take courage to do the right thing?

3. What obstacles keep you from being courageous to do the right thing?

4. Read 2 Chronicles 32:1–8. What steps did Hezekiah take in an effort to stand against Sennacherib?

Isn't it interesting that, like Deborah, Hezekiah didn't say, "We've fortified the walls and made plenty of weapons, so with our preparation and our skill, we should be able to defeat Sennacherib"? What an example to us. How often do we take the credit when the Lord delivers us from situations? What else or who else do we like to credit with our successes?

5. What reason does Hezekiah give the people to be courageous?

6. Read 2 Chronicles 32:16–21. Besides being courageous, what else did Hezekiah do that led to the annihilation of the Assyrian king?

7. How much fighting did the Israelites do?

8. Read 2 Chronicles 32:22–23. What benefits did Hezekiah and the people of Jerusalem enjoy thanks to Hezekiah's leading the people to courageously depend on God?

9. Think of how easy it would have been to lose faith in God while looking at a vast army that had conquered many other nations. We may not be staring at enemy combatants, but we lose hope in God, too, when we quit praying about issues or don't take them to God. Isn't it easier to complain about all that's wrong in our lives and to try to find a self-help solution or busy ourselves with all the battle preparations? Do we forget to fall before God in humility, confessing that the battle is His and that we desperately depend on Him?

RELUCTANCE

10. Read the following Scripture and write the Lord's response to reluctance in each scenario.

   Exodus 3:7–12; 4:10–14

   Jeremiah 1:6–10, 17

   Jonah 1:1–3, 11–16

11. What are some words that describe how God feels regarding reluctance to do His will?

12. Reluctance to do God's will might be especially annoying to Him given the promises He's given us. What are some of the promises He gives us that should curb our reluctance to do His will?

13. Read Acts 15:36–41. Reluctance to do God's will might disappoint more than God. Who else may our reluctance impact?

14. Read Numbers 13:27–33; 14:5–10, 20–24, 36–38. The spies who were reluctant to go into the land refused to let Caleb persuade them. What did their reluctance lead them to do (13:31–33)?

15. How did this impact the rest of the people (14:10)?

16. How did God deal with them (14:36–37)?

17. Joshua and Caleb were the only two who didn't show reluctance to go into the land God had promised them. What was their reward?

18. God's Word clearly shows a disdain for reluctance to do God's will. Have you been reluctant to work for the Lord? If so, why?

19. Now that you know God's heart regarding reluctance, how will you prioritize differently?

My reluctance usually comes about because (A) I can't decide whether it's really God's will to serve Him in that capacity; (B) I don't think I have time; (C) my sinful nature hopes that if I refrain long enough, someone else will step in so I don't have to; or (D) I don't think I'm qualified.

Regarding God's will, serving the Lord is almost always according to God's will. Why wouldn't it be? Having said that, I do much less during the summer when my kids are all home from school. My children need me, and I'm certain God is okay with my family being my priority during those times. However, I also know the Devil's evil army loves to keep me from serving. If something needs to go, there's a long list of other things I can cut back on to gain time.

In regard to time, it's good to evaluate your life to see where time is wasted. You'd be surprised at what you could accomplish by shutting off the TV, computer, or electronic device of your choice. Even if you were to serve in no other way, imagine the impact on countless lives praying for that half hour might have.

God tells us to "seek first His kingdom and all the rest will be given to you as well" (Matt. 6:33). When we do God's work, the rest gets done. God supplies the energy to do what needs to be done, someone steps in to help out, or we realize that what didn't get done wasn't so important. We may need to give things up.

As far as being qualified, in Romans 12, the apostle Paul urges us to use our bodies as living sacrifices. In that regard he tells us to use sober judgment. That judgment is going to help us evaluate where best to use our time and resources. There may be some trial and error to figure out what our strengths and weaknesses are.

TRUST

20. Read Daniel 3:13–18. What was Shadrach, Meshach, and Abednego's attitude about being thrown in the furnace (16–18)?

It's good for us to read this, because God doesn't always save His people. In Acts 7 we read about Stephen being stoned to death. Acts 12 reports that James was martyred, but Peter was spared. God has His own intentions and purposes for each life. How should this change our expectations and the way we pray?

21. Read Daniel 3:26–28. Why did Nebuchadnezzar say God had saved them (v. 28)?

22. Read Daniel 6:10–23. What reason does Scripture give us for why Daniel was spared (23)?

23. These are pretty big issues. These men faced death. Most of us don't face such big things day to day. What are the things you must trust God for each day?

24. Read Isaiah 30:15–21. What does the Lord ask the people to do (v. 15)?

25. What did the people choose to rely on instead of God (v. 16)?

26. What are some things we are tempted to rely on?

27. What would the Lord have given them in return for their repentance and trust (vv. 18–21)?

28. Read Genesis 18:10–14. To Sarah, infertility seemed too big of an issue for God. What situation in your life seems too big for you? Is that situation too big for God?

God's Word clearly shows God's hand working in the lives of believers. If you are struggling relationally, materially, physically, or emotionally, cling to Him, not to the fleeting comforts of this world.

SOMETHING TO THINK ABOUT

Did God ever provide for you in ways you didn't want? Maybe He provided you with a house you could afford, but you wanted a much bigger house. Maybe He provided you with hand-me-down clothes for your children, but you wanted name-brand clothes or a different style than what you were given. Maybe you wanted a car, but you got a bike instead, a bike that provided you a healthier lifestyle than a car would have. Maybe you prayed for the Lord to cure a loved one, but God took him or her home to heaven instead, where he or she would never suffer again.

Pray that you would see the answers to your prayers and accept them, trusting that God is always working for your good and giving you what you need, regardless of whether it fulfills your wants.

I have prayed and trusted many times that my prayers would be answered. I'm not always so quick to add what the three men in the fiery furnace added: "Even if You don't, I will still serve You."

Are you quick to bring glory to God and defend Him, even when He answers your prayers with a no?

Prayer to Close the Lesson:

The apostle Paul wrote to the Philippians that he eagerly expected and hoped that he would have sufficient courage so that Christ would be exalted in him (Phil. 1:20). Heavenly Father, give us the same sufficient courage so we may fulfill Your plans for our lives. Forgive us for the reluctance we have shown in obeying You. Forgive us for seeking and being content in our comfort while neglecting Your work. Lord, we do believe. Help us to overcome our unbelief. Help us to trust in all situations that You are in control and able to do abundantly more than we could ever ask or imagine. In Christ we pray. Amen.

LESSON FOUR

Ruth

READ RUTH 1:1–18; 2:1–3, 8–12, 23; 3:1–6, 10–14; 4:8–17.

Devotion: Ruth has a lot to teach us about being a Christian, despite the fact that she was born in a heathen and idolatrous nation. She is called a woman of noble character in Ruth 3:11, and it is worth looking closer at the qualities she has that define her as such so we can apply them to our lives.

From the first chapter, we learn that Ruth was widowed at presumably a young age and was without children. Her mother-in-law, Naomi, found herself alone in a foreign land at a not-so-young age and decided to return to her homeland. Before she left, she released Ruth and Orpah from any duty they had in regard to caring for her. At this time, Orpah returned to her family. There was nothing wrong with doing so. Ruth's decision, however, to stay and care for Naomi, to leave her family and everything familiar, and to take whatever came, whether remaining unmarried or finding a husband, was a more noble one.

Ruth was able to see past the undesirable events in her life to comfort and care for Naomi, who lost not only her husband, as Ruth had, but also her two sons. The Bible reveals that Naomi felt God had forsaken her with the deaths of her husband and two sons. "It is more bitter for me than for you," she told Ruth and Orpah, "because the Lord's hand has gone out against me" (1:13).

Upon returning home, she told her old friends, "Don't call me Naomi. Call me Mara because the Almighty has made my life very bitter. The Lord has afflicted me; the Almighty has brought misfortune upon me" (1:20–21).

Do you get the idea that this task of Ruth's was easy? Naomi was a woman who was rightfully distressed in spirit. All she had was taken away, and she couldn't find the silver lining.

Ruth faced Naomi's attitude with a resolute desire to care for her. "May the Lord deal with me, be it ever so severely, if anything but death separates you and me" (1:17). Ruth didn't take the easy way out, ditching Naomi and her attitude to go make a life for herself. When she got to Bethlehem, she didn't say, "Call me Mara, too. My husband's dead, I have no children, and here I am away from family and friends because someone has to look out for this old woman."

Without worrying about her own plans, Ruth took care of Naomi, working hard to bring food home for the two of them. She respected her mother-in-law and did what she asked.

"I will do whatever you say," Ruth answered Naomi when told to go to Boaz at night (3:5). How many of us, when getting advice on how to live our lives, respond to people with the same grace? Isn't it easier to present our argument on why we're doing what we're doing, to ignore the advice, or worse—nod politely and think, *Never in a million years*?

Whether Naomi was complaining or coming up with plans for Ruth's future, Ruth treated her with the utmost respect: serving Naomi, listening to her, and sharing all she had with her.

God was in control of all this, and Ruth's life shows a solid trust in placing herself totally in God's hands and relying on Him to provide. Boaz noticed this and blessed Ruth, saying, "May the Lord repay you for what you have done. May you be richly rewarded by the Lord, the God of Israel, under whose wings you have come to take refuge" (2:12).

God provided Boaz's field not only for food but for protection as well. Boaz told her, "My daughter, listen to me. Don't go and glean in another field and don't go away from here. Stay here with the women who work for me. Watch the field where the men are harvesting, and follow along after the women. I have told the men not to lay a hand on you. And whenever you are thirsty, go and get a drink from the water jars the men have filled" (2:8–9). Boaz told the men not to touch her, and he also told them, "Let her gather among the sheaves and don't reprimand her. Even pull out some stalks for her from the bundles and leave them for her to pick up, and don't rebuke her" (2:15–16).

God provided all Ruth needed and more. He took her husband, but He certainly didn't remove His blessing. Ruth went with willing hands and did what the Lord put before her, and He showed Ruth that He is merciful and loving and that He listens when we turn to Him to meet our needs.

In fact, Scripture shows that God is displeased when we don't come to Him for help. Isaiah 31:1 says, "Woe to those who go down to Egypt for help, who rely on horses, who trust in the multitude of their chariots and in the great strength of their horsemen, but do not look to the Holy One of Israel, or seek help for the Lord." And Psalm 146:3–6 says, "Do not put your trust in princes, in human beings, who cannot save. When their spirit departs, they return to the ground; on that very day their plans come to nothing. Blessed are those whose help is the God of Jacob, whose hope is in the Lord their God. He is the Maker of heaven and earth, the sea and everything in them—he remains faithful forever."

At the end of the account of Ruth, when Ruth had a son, the women of Bethlehem said, "Naomi has a son!"

Ruth truly was a woman of noble character. Her self-denial extended to sharing her son, even allowing him to be called Naomi's. It would only have been natural for Ruth to think Naomi had had her chance to raise two boys; now it was her turn to bask in motherhood, and no one would take even a hint of that away from her.

Whatever trials we face in life, may we face them with the same resolve to do what is right, even when it isn't easy or doesn't seem to be the most beneficial to us. God rewarded Ruth's self-denial, and that ultimately is the reward we should seek. Jesus said in Matthew 6:1, 3–4, "Be careful not to do your 'acts of righteousness' before men, to be seen by them. If you do, you will have no reward from your Father in heaven … But when you give to the needy, do not let your left hand know what your right hand is doing, so that your giving may be in secret. Then your Father, who sees what is done in secret, will reward you."

Devotion Question: Are you willing to sacrifice for those God put in your life? It's easy to fall into self-absorption and think only about our comforts and wants. Jesus said, "The Son of man did not come to be served, but to serve" (Matt. 20:28; Mark 10:45). His example should spur us to do the same.

How has self-absorption hindered your service to God and others?

Topics for further study:

OBEDIENCE

1. Read Genesis 22:15–18. What were the blessings that came as a result of Abraham's obedience?

2. Read Isaiah 1:19–20. What did God promise as the reward for obedience?

3. That didn't mean obedience would result in good meals and fine dining, although that was certainly part of it. What is included in the promise to eat the good things of the land?

4. Read 1 John 5:3. John could have said so many things here. He could have said, "This is love for God: to tell others about Him" or "to worship Him" or "to trust Him" or "to have unwavering faith." But John, inspired by the Holy Spirit, said that if we love God, we should show it with our obedience. What is that obedience going to look like in our lives?

5. Read 1 Timothy 5:4. How do we know that helping and loving our mother-in-law is part of obedience to God?

If you are a woman and you marry a man, you become part of his family, and he becomes part of yours. My mother has enjoyed the benefit of my husband's efforts on many occasions. My parents have helped us out in certain ways, and my husband's parents have helped us in others. The sooner you accept his family as your family and the sooner he accepts your family as his, the sooner you can all start the business of taking care of each other. That is one of the primary blessings of family. The Bible doesn't tell daughters-in-law to obey their mother-in-law. What should our relationship with our mother-in-law be?

The Ins and Outs of the Christian Family

6. Read Ephesians 6:1–3 and Colossians 3:20. What is a child's job in a family?

7. Why should children obey (Eph. 6:1; Col. 3:20)?

8. Which of his or her parents' requests should a child obey (3:20)?

9. What would be the exception (Acts 5:29)?

10. Read Colossians 3:18. What is the wife's role?

11. What things make it hard for a Christian wife to be submissive? Why is this such a struggle at times?

12. Read Colossians 3:19. What is the husband to do? What is he not to do?

13. Read Ephesians 6:4 and Colossians 3:21.What are parents to do?

14. What are parents not to do?

15. What might we inadvertently do that would embitter our children?

Have you ever had someone follow you, scrutinizing your every action? Sometimes I think parents fall into that trap, and it's not just a temptation for parents. We can do the same to a pastor, neighbor, sibling, or coworker.

In catechism classes we're taught that the Word acts like a mirror. As we look at God's perfect standard, we see our own failures. We don't love God with all our hearts. We don't show love to those who annoy or mistreat us. We don't pray for those who make our lives miserable. We break all the other commandments, too.

All too often we hold the mirror outwardly and look at others' faults and the ways they don't measure up.

Make a point to stop scrutinizing those around you. As you see their shortcomings, make sure you aren't doing the same things. Change your behavior and pray for others.

16. Look back at 1 Timothy 5:4. What is a child's role when a parent is left a widow?

17. Why should a child take care of a parent who has been widowed?

18. Read 1 Timothy 5:8. What other role do we have?

Paul tells us to provide for our relatives. It's easy to get caught up in working for a better life here on earth at the expense of having time to serve the Lord and the community. Who doesn't want a big, beautiful house? Who doesn't want a big-screen TV, new cars, or a super-clean, well-maintained apartment or house?

Providing for yourself or your family (immediate and extended) is just that: providing housing, food, clothing, and shoes. It's not wrong to have a career, and it's not wrong to have a job. We just want to make sure working doesn't become an excuse not to work in the church or for the Lord, and we want to make sure working for the Lord doesn't become an excuse for not taking care of our families.

THE FELLOWSHIP OF BELIEVERS

19. Read Hebrews 10:23–25. What does the writer of Hebrews admonish us to do in verse 23 that helps the family of believers?

20. How should we motivate each other to act?

21. When you give your Christian friends advice, do you motivate them to love, forgive, and go the extra mile, or do you tell them to respond as the world would—cut a person off, hold grudges, or retaliate with something equally hurtful?

22. What two things does verse 25 urge us to do?

23. Certainly this includes meeting together for worship but not exclusively. What are some other ways we can get together to encourage one another?

24. Read Galatians 6:9–10. Paul tells us to do good to all people, especially believers. Think of specifics. How can we do good to others?

This puts the burden of the church on all of us. Take note of when people are in need, not just in your church but in your community, too; organize ways to help out. It's the responsibility of each of us to care for one another.

SOMETHING TO THINK ABOUT

More than once, when I've been overwhelmed while trying to get things together for an event at church or a special occasion for my family, my sisters in Christ have rebuked me for not calling on them for help. Do you ignore or refuse the help others in the body of Christ would readily offer? If so, why?

Prayer to Close the Lesson:

Beloved Lord, Thank You for our brothers and sisters in Christ who support us, encourage us, and remind us of Your love. Fill the voids in our family lives. Where there has been dissention, bring unity; where there has been strife, bring peace. Give us obedient hearts set to serve You. Thank You for all You've done for us and continue to do for us. In Jesus's name we pray. Amen.

LESSON FIVE

Naomi

READ RUTH 1:1–22; 4:13–17.

Devotion: Can't we all relate to Naomi? When trouble comes our way, it can be easy to blame God. In fact, we even blame God when our own shortcomings get us in trouble.

This attitude arrived with our sinful nature. After Adam and Eve sinned, Eve blamed the serpent, but Adam blamed God. He said, "The woman *you put here* with me—she gave me some of the fruit from the tree and I ate it" (Gen. 3:12, emphasis added). In other words: "It's Your fault, God. You put her here. If she hadn't been here, I wouldn't be in this situation."

Naomi's situation didn't come about because of her sin but because of the curse of sin. Romans 6:23 says, "The wages of sin is death." Death, destruction, and deterioration are part of life thanks to sin. Paul says all of creation groans beneath the weight of sin (Rom. 8:22). It isn't just us. The animals, nature, and the earth itself suffer because of the curse of sin.

God could have let us live here forever, but He didn't want this to be our forever home. He wanted to bring us to a place of perfection, without suffering. And that means we have to die.

But did God really need to take Naomi's husband and both of her sons? We have the gift of seeing the end of this account, so we can see God's plan to bring Ruth and Boaz together. We see from the text how godly they were—and God desired that godliness in the great-grandparents of King David, "a man after God's own heart" (1 Sam. 13:14).

Naomi was God's chosen vehicle to bring Ruth and Boaz together, but this union would come about only through pain.

Right now you may be saying, "Thanks very much, Lord, but I'll pass on being Your chosen vehicle. I don't need that."

If you had told Joseph what he would have to endure for God to use him, he likely wouldn't have signed up for it. I'm fairly certain Esther wouldn't have chosen to be orphaned, to be forced into the king's harem, or to be taken to the king to give up her virginity. I doubt Daniel's dream was to be taken from his home and homeland and to serve in a heathen court, where his dedication to God had him continually being the odd man out. Would Ezekiel have willingly given up his wife to be the sign for Israel?

Don't misunderstand. Service to God isn't just pain and drama. God is in the business of restoration. Joseph got his family back, only better. The jealousy and hatred of the past were replaced with forgiveness and love as Joseph brought his family to Egypt. Daniel was at the top of his game, and God gave him devout friends to share his journey. Esther was made queen. She had maids and luxury at her fingertips. These servants of God enjoyed influence in their day, but even more importantly, they finished strong and are enjoying their heavenly reward.

We see restoration at the end of Naomi's account, too. Ruth proved to be "better than seven sons," and there was new life in the family again. And that was only the beginning, because as the last verses reminded us, this was the beginning of the royal line that would forever represent Israel.

How do we go through trials without becoming bitter or resenting God? Naomi was right after all, that everything had passed through God's hand before coming to her. And didn't she have a right to be bitter after what she'd gone through?

During hard times, we need to go back to the character and promises of God. From His Word, we know God loves us so much that He sent His Son to die for us (John 3:16). He keeps track of every hair on our heads (Matt. 10:30). He's sovereign, and His prophecies have proved true hundreds and sometimes thousands of years before things happened. He's compassionate, as shown through Jesus, the manifestation of God the Father, who showed great compassion. He's trustworthy and has kept all His promises. He has promised to take care of us (Matt. 6), to keep track of us (Isa. 49:16), and to work all things for our good (Rom. 8:28).

God isn't a sadistic entity out to cause us grief and pain. He's a loving Father, watching out for us, caring for us, and molding and shaping us.

God looks at us and our situation through eternal eyes. Taking a believer to heaven is a gift to be celebrated, even if it comes earlier than we hoped. We prefer to hold on to those we love and for life to unfold according to our plans, but God's ways are higher than ours, and in times when we don't understand, we need to trust God's character and promises. We lean into those instead of our own sinful and flawed thoughts and emotions.

Devotion Question: Do you have a tendency to hold onto people and things too tightly? I did, especially when my children were young. I wanted to control who was in their life and keep adversity from them.

As they get older, I struggle with worry. I have to remind myself to trust God when my children are in situations out of my control. As hard as it is, I must hand things off to God and pray for Him to carry what I can't.

It helps when I imagine myself as a small child struggling to carry a heavy bag of groceries. God is like that loving parent that rushes over to take hold of the bag and easily carries it.

What worry is burdening you right now? Are you ready to give it to God?

Let God take your burden for you. He can handle it.

Topics for further study:

BITTERNESS

1. Read Romans 3:10–18. The apostle Paul described the power of our sinful nature. By nature what traits do we possess (vv. 13–18)?

   To paraphrase, we practice _____ (v. 13), we _____ (v. 14), and are _____ (v. 14). We shed _____ (v. 15) and don't know _____ (v. 17). We don't _____ God (v. 18).

   Right now you might be saying, "That's not me!" But if you're honest, it is. Haven't you exaggerated (practiced deceit) and wished someone would be destroyed (damned to hell)? Hasn't jealousy ever driven you to pick someone apart? We may not draw blood, but we use our tongues as swords, cutting people down. We worry, and we forget to give God the time and honor He deserves. We are woefully slaves to our sinful natures.

2. Read 1 Kings 8:37–40. Solomon made a point to mention in his prayer those who call out to God with afflictions of the heart. What quality does the image of someone spreading his or her hands toward the temple portray?

3. Read Daniel 6:10–11. Daniel knew the verses in 1 Kings 8:38–40. What was he doing when he opened his windows toward Jerusalem and got down on his knees?

4. What is the difference between falling on your face before God with outstretched hands, begging Him to pick you up, and shaking a fist at God, asking Him, "How dare you"?

5. To be human means we will experience afflictions of the heart. The way we respond to those afflictions shows the condition of our hearts. What are some normal feelings during times of distress?

6. What are some sinful responses to pain in our lives?

7. Read Ephesians 4:31. What did Paul tell us to do in regard to bitterness, rage, anger, and slander?

It's interesting that Paul made this a command. Elsewhere he made suggestions, but here he commanded us to get rid of *all* bitterness and rage. That doesn't leave us much room for hanging onto bitterness, does it? Bitterness typically arises when we feel someone has wronged us.

Sometimes we resent another person for the way he or she treated us in the past. Paul went on to say in Ephesians 4:32, "Be kind and compassionate toward one another, forgiving each other, just as in Christ, God forgave you." The parable of the unmerciful servant reminds us of our great debt, which Christ's death canceled, and it leads us to forgive one another as well.

To be bitter toward God means we don't believe He is loving, kind, or just in His treatment of us. Or perhaps we feel He's lost sight of us altogether. The promises from His Word assure us that this isn't the case.

Are you holding onto bitterness in some area of your life?

8. When we are hurt or troubled over a situation, what can we do to keep from becoming bitter?

THE PROPER WAY TO DEAL WITH LOSS

9. Read Luke 7:11–15. What did Jesus feel when He saw the mother of the dead boy (v. 13)?

10. Read John 11:32–35. What did Mary do when she saw Jesus?

11. What did Jesus feel when He saw Mary's grief?

12. Read Isaiah 63:9. How can this passage comfort us when we are reeling from a loved one's death or another crisis?

13. Read Psalm 116:15. What word does God use to describe the death of a believer?

14. That's not a word we typically associate with death. How might that word put a new spin on the diagnosis of terminal cancer or another disease or even of the death of a young person?

15. Read 1 Thessalonians 4:13–18. The whole of Christianity relies on the belief that Jesus died for our sins to pay our debt so we might be with Him in heaven. The apostle Paul didn't say we can't grieve. He told us not to lose hope in our grief. What's the difference?

16. Read John 14:1–3. Break this verse down as a practical application for how to grieve. Jesus said to not let our hearts be _____ but to _____ God, because we are going to be with Him in _____.

This means our grief shouldn't overcome us, because as Christians, we are assured of a future and a hope. Soon we will all be together in heaven with Christ and our loved ones.

17. On the flip side of this, when is there no comfort to be found when a friend or loved one dies?

18. How should this change the way we live?

How to Be a Friend to the Grieving

19. Read Ruth 1:15–17. What is one thing Ruth did for Naomi while Naomi was grieving?

20. Is that what Naomi said she wanted?

21. What does that tell you about being with someone in the days, weeks, and months after a loved one has died or when someone is in crisis?

22. Read Ruth 2:2. What practical need did Ruth supply?

23. Read Romans 12:15. How can we be a good friend to someone during his or her dark days?

24. How can we mourn with him or her without falling into despair?

25. Read Ruth 1:19–21; 4:13–14. On what occasions did the women of the town come to Ruth?

26. It's important to walk with our friends through the stages of life. You may not always be able to be physically present. What can you do when you can't be with them?

SOMETHING TO THINK ABOUT

Dr. James Dobson said there are two kinds of people in the world: those who are suffering and those who will suffer. Jesus said, "In this world you will have trouble" (John 16:33).

I once heard of a man who was diagnosed with terminal cancer while he was in the prime of his life. He had a good job and a family with fairly young children. His prayer from the beginning was that through the cancer he would glorify God. And he did. Until the day he went home to be with the Lord, he reminded and reassured his friends and family of the goodness of God.

When troubles come your way, do you ask that your life and actions would glorify God? Do you consider the example you can be to the world in the midst of your struggle?

Prayer to Close the Lesson:

Heavenly Father, prepare us for the days ahead. Give us the tools to deal with what You have planned for us. Let us never fall away from You, but let our lives glorify You and bring honor to Your name. Remove every hint of bitterness from us and replace it with trust in You. Hear us because of Your Son. Amen.

Lesson Six

Abigail

Read 1 Samuel 25:1–44.

Devotion: The Bible describes Nabal as a wealthy man who was mean and surly (which means bad tempered and rude), but it refers to Abigail as beautiful and intelligent. When the Bible describes a person, it's good for us to take note. Only three other women—Sarah (Gen. 12:14), Rachel (Gen. 29:17), and Esther (Est. 2:7)—are described as beautiful, and none of the others are also listed as intelligent.

How is it that this beautiful, intelligent woman ended up with such a mean man? In Abigail's day, marriages were arranged, so a woman like Abigail, who had much to offer, would have brought a great price. Likely Nabal was able to marry her because of his wealth. How unfortunate that Abigail's father didn't do as Abraham had when he sent his servant a great distance to ensure his child had a godly spouse.

Because we have a choice, seeking godliness in a future spouse is important to stress. Radio speaker Debbie Griffith talked about this in her segment, *Everyday Matters*.[5] She compared looking for a spouse to house hunting. She warned that we can get caught up in cosmetics and layouts, and miss a cracked foundation.

Jesus said a man who listens to God and puts God's Word into practice is like a man who builds his house on a rock. That foundation is secure (Matt. 7:24–27). It's a blessing for a godly woman to weather the storms of life with a man who looks to God for his strength. That's not to say that godly men don't come with shortcomings or that a marriage to a godly man will be easy. We all struggle with sin and selfish expectations, and every marriage will require work. Godly men can struggle with possessing a sharp tongue, pride, or hastiness; being impatient or demeaning; and having a lack of self-control, just as unbelievers do. But blessed indeed is the couple who can pray together, even after a horrible day.

When Nabal acted foolishly, Abigail made a split-second decision to save her household. Commentator Matthew Henry pointed out that by not submitting to Nabal's wishes in this instance, Abigail submitted to what was in his best interest. To not

---

[5] Debbie Griffith is from MN and her radio segment, "Everyday Matters" airs throughout the midwest. For more information about Debbie visit www.debbiegriffith.com.

act would have meant certain death for him and all those in his household.[6]

Godly submission doesn't mean sitting by and letting the house or workplace fall into ruin. It means that if a husband prefers not to do family devotions and prayers, the wife does them. If he doesn't help the children with their homework, the wife does the task. It means if our boss isn't well mannered and we are capable, we act on our boss's behalf to preserve his or her good name and honor. Acting this way typically brings respect, not reproach. When we see something that could positively affect the business, most employers are happy to have someone step in. That sort of independent thinking is what separates the person who is there to put in his or her time from the dedicated employee.

Abigail had to deal with two difficult men. Nabal was indignant, yes, but David's temper got the best of him, too. Abigail's gift offered a generous supply of food and equally generous words to calm David's temper and cover her husband's rude actions.

Defusing situations often requires a level head to deal with difficult people and issues on both sides. When we're told about a conflict, we can encourage a person to respond in love and forgiveness, or we can spur the person's anger, leading him or her down a road of sin with harmful thoughts and actions regarding the other person. We can advise others to seek peace and compromise or to hold grudges. Difficult people are everywhere, and all of us

[6] "Matthew Henry's complete commentary on the Bible 1 Samuel 25," StudyLight.org, accessed February 2015, (http://www.studylight.org/com/mhm/view.cgi?book=1sa&chapter=025)

will have them in our lives at some point. It may be a coworker or manager, the person who rides your bus, a neighbor, or even someone at church whose personality clashes with yours.

After saving her household, Abigail didn't go straight to her husband and demand to know what he was thinking and whether he knew the ramifications of his actions. Confronting Nabal in front of his servants during sheering wouldn't merely have been demeaning to him; it probably would have brought his retaliation on Abigail. Confronting anyone whose actions or words are less than ideal will require tact, wisdom, and a pure heart on our part. It always helps to remember our own shortcomings. Then we can approach the other person in humility and with grace ask him or her to consider a different approach.

We also see from this account that even when a person refuses to see his or her sin or treats others poorly, we don't need to seek revenge or cause fights. The Lord sees everything. Romans 12:19 tells us, "Do not take revenge, my dear friends, but leave room for God's wrath, for it is written: 'It is mine to avenge; I will repay,' says the Lord."

Our role is found in Leviticus 19:18, where God tells His people, "Do not seek revenge or bear a grudge against anyone among your people, but love your neighbor as yourself. I am the Lord."

It isn't necessary for us to keep score with the person who makes our lives miserable. The Lord sees our thoughts and actions, and He rewards and chastises as He sees fit. If we harbor ill feelings toward anyone who has sinned against us, we are equally guilty of sin. Jesus said in Matthew 6:14–15, "For if you forgive men when they sin against you, your heavenly Father will also forgive you. But if you do not forgive men their sins your Father will not forgive your sins."

Many people in society and even in the church would encourage the "Abigails" to get away from a husband whose words are thoughtless and whose actions are hasty. But a pure heart and righteous spirit lead us to stay, to put out the fires of a "Nabal's" wickedness as they arise, and to depend on God.

Lest we romanticize that Nabal's death and Abigail's subsequent marriage to David was her "happily ever after," we'd do well to remember that David eventually married other wives and took concubines, too. Six wives are listed in 2 Samuel 3:2–5, and 2 Samuel 5:13 tells us he took more concubines and wives, and that was before Bathsheba. My guess is that Abigail's days of defusing stressful situations didn't end with Nabal.

When we trust God for the strength to overcome difficult situations and lead a life of love, we can be sure God will reward us in His time. Even if we are in a difficult relationship for as long as a parent, sibling, spouse, boss, or whoever lives, we can be assured that living in love will be rewarded in eternity. That's our "happily ever after."

Devotion Question: Mark 10:9 says, "What God has joined together, let no man separate." When a friend calls to complain about her husband, do you readily agree that he's half the man he ought to be, or do you listen and empathize, reminding her of her husband's strengths and the blessing he is to her while encouraging her to serve, forgive, and submit? Do you pray for her husband for the sake of her marriage?

Topics for further study:

GOD'S HEART TOWARD DIVORCE

1. Read Matthew 19:4–6. What are God's intentions for marriage?

   A.

   B.

   C.

2. Read Matthew 19:7–9. What does Jesus say causes most divorce?

   A hard heart is one that refuses to try anymore. It's the person who has had enough, who doesn't want to serve, forgive, or overlook. It's a heart that wants the freedom to think only of itself: my wants, my needs, my happiness.

3. Matthew 19:9 gives us one acceptable reason for divorce. What is it?

4. Read 1 Corinthians 7:15. What is another reason for which God allows divorce?

I've heard people say a spouse emotionally deserted or committed adultery. While it is true that some spouses have an emotional deficit and that becoming emotionally connected to another person is a form of adultery, such excuses typically come from people who are eager to find what they consider a legitimate reason for divorce. If you're looking for that, then your heart is in the wrong place. It would be better instead to put your energy into praying for your spouse, your marriage, and your heart.

5. Read Malachi 2:13–16. What does a godly marriage produce (v. 15)?

6. Why is God concerned about godly offspring?

7. What was God no longer doing because of divorce and unfaithfulness (v. 13)?

8. What does God expect of the husband?

9. What can we do to encourage married couples?

10. What can we do to encourage single or widowed people to honor God and marriage in the way they live?

SUBMISSION

Submission in marriage is often misunderstood. It's important for us to understand what submission is in marriage whether married or single so we're able to explain it to others and to help and encourage our friends and others to do what is right for their marriage.

11. Read Ephesians 5:22–24. How much is a wife to submit to her husband (v. 24)?

12. This language or idea isn't going to get applause in secular circles, but God doesn't give wives any disclaimers. He doesn't say, "Wives, if your husband is godly, submit to him in everything." In light of what we talked about in our devotion, what should a Christian woman do when she disagrees with her husband?

The fundamental factor is motivation. Grasping for power is going to look very different than acting on our husband's behalf.

13. Read 1 Peter 3:1–6. Of what benefit is it for a woman to be submissive to her husband?

    A. From verse 1:

    B. From verse 4:

14. How does the world see beauty (v. 3)?

15. What qualities does the Lord find beautiful in a woman (v. 4)?

16. Read Genesis 20. Where did Sarah end up after submitting to Abraham?

17. In verse 11 Abraham made the assumption that there "is surely no fear of God in this place." Was that assumption accurate? What is the irony of that statement?

18. What all did God do to rescue Sarah from that situation? I see three things.

19. Now go back to Genesis 16 and read verses 1–6. Sarah decided to take charge. God had promised them children, but they weren't having any. What was her solution?

20. How did Hagar feel once she was pregnant (v. 4)?

21. What did Sarah do once she was despised (v. 6)?

22. Hagar ran away from Sarah, and in verses 7–12, we see that God intervened. What was His advice to Hagar (v. 9)?

23. What would she get in return (v. 10)?

When Sarah submitted, God rescued her. When Sarah took charge and came up with the solution that seemed best to her, havoc ensued. When Hagar submitted, God promised to make her descendants great. This promise should encourage us as we determine to submit to those in our lives God has put over us. God won't lose sight of us.

Have you ever been in a situation where there were too many cooks in the kitchen? Or have you been in a situation where no one would take charge? Either situation can be chaotic. Typically businesses and organizations have a chain of command, which in the best of situations equates to everyone working together and doing his or her job peacefully for the sake of the business or organization. All employment situations experience conflict or turmoil at some point, and it's up to the person in charge to determine the action. Often if a boss trusts the employee, he or she is fine with whatever course of action the employee takes. Other times require meetings, research, debate, and someone to make the final decision.

Marriage is a lot like that. A wise couple will look at the tasks at hand and determine who is best at dealing with each and work together for the good of the home. A godly couple also remembers that in all situations we all submit to the Lord, and ultimately the goal is to serve the Lord together, making the most of our strengths and helping each other through the weaknesses.

24. Regardless of whether we are married, all of us must submit to people. Read Romans 13:1–7. Paul talked about those who govern. Why is it important that we be reminded to submit to those who hold office at the local, state, and national levels?

25. What are those whom God put over us supposed to be doing (vv. 4, 6)?

26. Why is verse 1 important for us to remember?

Submission means humbling ourselves to another's authority. Respect is the attitude in which we submit. It is possible to submit without showing respect. We do this when we say, "Fine. Have it your way!" and stomp away or agree to submit while mumbling in our hearts. If we truly respect those in authority, however, submission isn't a chore.

My wise grandma taught me a lesson years ago when she told me my job was to submit and not to worry about the outcome. Those in authority will stand before God for their actions and decisions. God has asked us to submit. When a situation is out of our hands and isn't life or death or against God's will, we must submit and let God deal with the rest.

27. Read Acts 5:29. When should we refuse to submit to someone over us?

Right now you may say, "Hold on! Abraham asked Sarah to lie, and lying is a sin! Not only that, but he put her life, or at least her purity on the line. She should have refused." And yet the Bible tells us to submit, just like Sarah did.

Motives seem to play a part in the situation. In Acts 5, we see Ananias and Sapphira lying to the church in an effort to bring glory and honor to themselves. God's judgment was swift and severe. On the contrary, in Exodus 1 we see the midwives lying to Pharaoh to save the Hebrew boys they were ordered to kill, and God blessing them for this deed (vv. 15–21). In Joshua 2, Rahab lied to the king and saved the lives of the two spies.

Abraham felt his life was in jeopardy and made a decision to act to save his life. Was it a good decision? No. He didn't trust in God's ability to save him. But Sarah was willing to be put in a harem to save her husband's life, if need be.

The midwives and Rahab saved lives by refusing to submit. Sarah tried to save a life through her submission.

28. Can you think of any situation in the Bible, other than this one, where someone refused to submit to something because it was obviously in violation of God's law?

LOOKING OUTSIDE YOUR OWN SITUATION

29. Read Matthew 14:1–14. What did Jesus do when He heard about John's death? Why?

30. What did He do when He saw the people? Why?

31. It is easy to wallow in our own situation and become self-absorbed. Why is it important not only to think about our needs, time, and families, but also the needs of others?

32. Read Acts 20:32-35. Paul first makes the point that he isn't coveting others' things. Why is that a factor in helping others?

33. Read 1 Corinthians 12:27-31. Paul not only supplied his needs, but the needs of others. It seems it should go without saying, but Paul is asking those who are fit and strong to give consideration to those who are weak. In what ways can a person be weak?

Can you imagine cutting your foot and deciding not to clean and bandage it? Or can you imagine caring only for your hands but not for your eyes, ears, or arms? That would be absurd. We need to take care of each other as part of the body of Christ. Some are gifted at sending notes of encouragement. Some are good at making meals. Some have money, and some have time. First, we need to remember that we're part of a body. Then we need to recognize what we can do so we can serve others.

34. Read 1 Timothy 5:16. What does this passage tell us about helping others?

As we help others, we have less time and energy to feel sorry for ourselves, and more time to realize how abundant God's blessing is in our lives. If life is getting you down, reach out to help someone who is going through a rough time. You will be a blessing to him or her, and you'll be blessed, too.

Something to Think About

The Bible talks a lot about arrogance and humility. We're encouraged to be completely humble and serve, using Jesus as our example.

Pride creeps into our lives in subtle ways. It appears in the mask of always thinking we're right or refusing to accept another person's advice, even guessing the motive for unsolicited advice ("They're just jealous!").

Humility is required for submission. What are some other ways pride sneaks into our lives, making it hard for us to submit to our employers, pastors, church leaders, or government officials?

Prayer to Close the Lesson:

Dear Father in heaven, give us the wisdom and tact to deal with the tough situations and people in our lives. Give us also a generous dose of perseverance so we can endure all we need to endure. Remind us that our days of "happily ever after" lie ahead, but while here on earth, we will be in battle. Help us to submit to those You have put over us. Let our words and actions point to You so we can win others to You just as Jesus did during His life. The kingdom, power, and glory are Yours now and forever. Amen.

Lesson Seven

The Queen of Sheba

READ 1 KINGS 10:1–13; MATTHEW 12:42.

Devotion: Pilate asked Jesus, "What is truth?" Each generation seems wise in its own eyes, but the next generation disproves much of what the former generation thought to be true.

Worldly philosophies are often in opposition to God's Word. They are tools Satan uses to strip honor and majesty from God and to fool unbelievers, and sometimes believers, into living contrary to the Word. Worldly philosophies feed our sinful nature. They proudly explain away God's ideas and propose better methods.

The Bible tells us the world's philosophies are foolish and will come to nothing. The apostle Paul asked, "Where is the wise man? Where is the scholar? Where is the philosopher of this age? Has not God made foolish the wisdom of the world?" (1 Cor. 1:20). And later Paul said, "We do speak a message of wisdom among the mature, but not the wisdom of this age or of the rulers of this age, who are coming to nothing" (1 Cor. 2:6).

Worldly philosophy points away from God and directs our attention to ourselves or others. It lies and says we can solve our own problems. If only we examine and know ourselves or this method, and believe in ourselves or this philosophy, we can do anything.

The Bible tells us that if we look to ourselves, we will find sin. Jesus said, "For out of the heart come evil thoughts, murder, adultery, sexual immorality, theft, false testimony, slander" (Mt. 15:19). Romans 1:21 says "For although they knew God, they neither glorified him as God nor gave thanks to him, but their thinking became futile and their foolish hearts were darkened." Evil, futile, and foolish ... That is the wisdom our sinful nature produces, and we are totally incapable of overcoming it on our own.

The queen of Sheba sought wisdom and went to Solomon. She heard his wisdom and praised God. Worldly wisdom points to men and directs our praise and admiration there. True wisdom points you to the Creator to praise Him.

Seeking wisdom is a noble goal, but like the queen of Sheba, we must be careful to go to the right place to get it. The apostle Paul warned us, "See to it that no one takes you captive through hollow and deceptive philosophy which depends on human tradition and the basic principles of this world rather than on Christ" (Col. 2:8).

If you're going to the TV, movies, magazines, and pop culture for advice and tips on living, you're likely to find hollow and deceptive philosophy. Far too often the views of our favorite daytime talk show host, a character on a TV drama or a famous musician shape our ideologies.

If you want wisdom, you must go to the Word. There you will find "the full riches of complete understanding, in order that [you] may know the mystery of God, namely Christ, in whom are hidden all the treasures of wisdom and knowledge" (Col. 2:2–3).

When we're troubled, it's easy to run away or turn to temporary but fleeting philosophies to get us through the day. It is so much better to fall before the throne of God, asking for wisdom to deal with our troubles in a godly way. Our troubles may not immediately disappear. Sometimes God uses troubles to shape our thinking and help us become spiritually mature, attaining fruits of the Spirit. God's will is that we would turn to Him for the answer to "unsearchable things we do not know" (Jer. 33:3), so when He answers us, the glory is His.

Devotion Question: When Job's life took a turn for the worse, his friends showed up to accuse and offer their "wisdom." Even Job's wife told Job to curse God and die. How do we know whether the advice offered to us, whether by Christians or unbelievers, is godly?

Topics for Further Study:

WHAT IS WISDOM?

My dictionary defines *wisdom* as "good judgment.[7]" Another definition is "the ability to discern or judge what is true, right or lasting."[8]

1. Read Numbers 23:19. Which attribute of God assures us His Word is true?

2. What phrase did Jesus use in John 6:53?

3. The phrase "I tell you the truth" is used twenty-eight times throughout the book of John. In John 14:6, Jesus didn't say He was telling the truth. What did He say?

4. Read John 8:44. If Jesus is truth, there is nothing false about Him. Contrast this with the Devil. What characteristics describe him?

5. If someone were to ask you why Jesus was born, what answer would you give? In John 18:37, Jesus told Pilate the reason He was born. What was that reason?

---

[7] Webster's New World Dictionary, 3rd College ed., s.v. "wisdom."

[8] Farlex,"*TheFreeDictionary.com*," Accessed March 2015 http://www. thefreedictionary.com/wisdom

In Matthew 8:17;12:17; 21:4; John 12:38; 13:18; and 15:25, the phrase "This was to fulfill the scripture or what was written" is used. That is just a few of the times the writers of the Gospels pointed out the prophecies Jesus fulfilled. Jesus fulfilled all the prophecies. These fulfillments validate that God the Father does what He says He will do. They are proof that God isn't a liar.

6. Read Daniel 4:37. God made Nebuchadnezzar to live like a beast of the field. He was humbled for not acknowledging God. When his sanity was restored, what characteristics of God did he proclaim?

7. Read 2 Thessalonians 1:3–10. It doesn't always seem like God is just. When we go through trials or persecutions, like the Christians in Thessalonica, things don't seem fair. But Paul saw the persecution as a blessing, first for what it produced in the Thessalonians. What growth did Paul see (vv. 3–4)?

8. It is possible that God, who is just, allows "unfair" or troubling events in our lives for our spiritual growth. But Paul also gave the believers hope. He said justice would prevail. How and when?

9. Read Revelation 15:3–4. Write down the characteristics of God listed in the song the seven angels sang.

It's good to look up the definitions of these words to see how they differ. The word *just* means "right or fair." *Holy* means "spiritually pure or sinless." *Righteous* means "acting in an upright manner."[9]

10. Read 1 Peter 1:22–25. What characteristic of God and His Word does this passage point out?

Read Ecclesiastes 3:14. There's very little we do that will last long. We cut our hair, and it retains its shape for four to eight weeks. We change the oil in our cars, and we're good for three months. We paint a room in our house, and it looks good for five to ten years if we're lucky. Our bodies have no guarantee of lasting another hour, day, or year. What a contrast to God's work. "Everything God does will endure forever. Nothing can be added to it and nothing taken from it."

If *wisdom* is defined as "insightful understanding of what is true, right and lasting," (see footnote on page 76) the above passages show us that God and His Word are true, right, and enduring. If we want to be wise, we need to seek God and His Word.

HOW DO WE OBTAIN WISDOM?

11. Read Proverbs 9:10. What does it mean to fear the Lord?

---

[9] Webster's New World Dictionary, 3rd College ed., s.v. "just," "holy," "righteous."

12. Read 1 Corinthians 1:17–2:16. If we're looking for wisdom, Paul tells us where we won't find it. We won't find it in the following:

A. _____ (v. 20)

B. _____ (v. 25)

C. _____ (1:26; 2:6)

True wisdom isn't the wisdom of this world (in other words, worldly philosophies). The wisdom of man (v. 25) speaks not only of worldly philosophy but also of the wisdom we'd find within ourselves in the self-help and humanist approach. Those of influence who rule the Internet, radio, and TV gladly spew philosophies that sound logical but are mostly contrary to true wisdom found in God's Word.

13. In which two places can wisdom be found?

A. _____ (2.10–11)

B. _____ (2:16)

14. Read Luke 11:13. How do we get the Spirit?

15. Read Acts 8:9–23. What might hinder us from receiving the Holy Spirit?

16. Read John 1:1–4; 1 John 5:13–14. How do we get access to the mind of Christ?

Have you ever wished you could sit down and have a conversation with Jesus so you could get answers to what's troubling you? You can every hour of every day—in fact, every time you open your Bible and pray in His name.

17. Read Proverbs 11:2. What else do we need to do to gain wisdom?

18. Why is humility such an important step in becoming wise?

19. Read James 3:13–18. How do you know whether a person's wisdom is from the Lord or is worldly? What characteristics will you see in that person's life?

THE ROLE AND RESPONSIBILITY OF THE WISE

20. Read 1 Kings 3:5–13. Of all the things Solomon could have asked for, he chose discernment. Who would benefit from this request?

21. Look at God's response in verses 10–13. Why was God pleased with Solomon's request?

22. Think of the things you ask of God. Do you typically ask God for things that benefit you or others? When Solomon asked for wisdom, a whole nation benefitted, even the queen of Sheba, who came from a distance. Which spiritual gifts have you asked for lately so you might benefit others?

23. Read 2 Samuel 15:12; 16:23. What was one of Absalom's strategies in trying to take the throne from his father, David?

24. Read 2 Samuel 15:31. What was David's strategy?

25. Read 2 Samuel 16:20–22; 17:1–4. Ahithophel had been David's trusted adviser. How did he use his judgment now?

26. Read 2 Samuel 15:32–34; 17:5–14. What was Hushai's role in the rebellion?

27. Up until Absalom's rebellion, David highly regarded Ahithophel's word. Read 1 Chronicles 27:33. Ahithophel was a wise man, but God used Hushai in the midst of the rebellion to work for David's good. Ahithophel was listed as the king's counselor, and Hushai also made the list of David's overseers. What was Hushai listed as?

28. In the end Ahithophel tried to use his wisdom to the detriment of others, but Hushai made himself available for God to use and

is listed as David's friend. Read 2 Samuel 17:23. Make a list of the similarities between Ahithophel and Judas.

29. What does this teach us about using our gifts, friends, and positions?

SOMETHING TO THINK ABOUT

Everything God gave us has a purpose. It may be for our benefit, but it may also be for the benefit of others, both in God's family and outside of it. Think of your gifts, talents, abilities, and possessions. Are you using these for your benefit, or are you graciously using them to further and build up the kingdom of believers and as a means of bringing glory to God's name in the unbelieving world? Make a list of things you can do to use your gifts, time, and ability better.

Prayer to Close the Lesson:

Forgive us, Lord, for being wise in our own eyes. Forgive us for so often seeking answers from people who know nothing about You. Forgive us for thinking we are somehow the solution to life's problems. Help us to crave and seek You. You have promised that when we seek You, we will find You. Give us Your Spirit to handle life's problems with the wisdom You give. Be our refuge and strength, our very great reward. We pray this in Jesus' name. Amen.

LESSON EIGHT

Esther

READ ESTHER 2:1–18; 3:8–15; 4:1–17.

Devotion: For some reason the account of Esther is often romanticized. If we take an honest look, however, we discover that Esther didn't have an easy road. She was orphaned, and her cousin, Mordecai, took her in. When Xerxes' edict was issued, she was "taken to the king's palace" (2:8). This wasn't a beauty contest she volunteered for, with the hope that she might get a shot at being queen. Mordecai spent his free time pacing back and forth, waiting for word on how she was doing (2:11). At the palace she was placed in the king's harem, not the place a godly Jew would have wanted a young lady in his care.

Lest we neglect to understand what kind of man Xerxes was, a careful look at the first two chapters of the book of Esther shows he was a man who spent over half a year showing everyone how rich he was. He was a man prone to drunkenness (1:7), and he made a rash decision to do away with his wife because he listened to his nobles (who acted less than noble) when his wife refused to be an object of his drunken lust in front of his men. When these same men came up with the idea to confiscate all the beautiful young ladies of the land, he was eager to listen. After a year of beauty treatments, each of these young girls came to him in the evening and returned in the morning. He tried them out sexually, then placed them in his harem and sent for the next girl. Xerxes was a man who worried about what the men around him thought, but he put no thought into taking daughters from their families and taking these girls' futures from them.

This heathen man was the man Esther married. He was a playboy, maybe a good catch for someone without religious convictions, but he wasn't what Mordecai or Esther would have hoped for.

Despite this, Esther exhibited extraordinary wisdom at a young age. When her time came to go to the king, she could have adorned herself however she wanted. Instead, she entrusted that decision to Hegai, the king's eunuch (2:15). To allow Hegai to pick out her things was to submit her wants to the king's.

Oh, for such a willing spirit, to be a person who is quick to consider others' desires above her own, even when the others we're considering are disagreeable, selfish, rash, or rude. Exhibiting unselfishness at home, in the grocery store, in our vehicles, and in the workplace would be noticeable and such a contrast from the norm. What a sweet fragrance we'd leave if this was how we operated throughout our day.

How different, too, our prayer life would be if we submitted our will to God's. Imagine if we asked only for things to benefit His kingdom. Imagine the difference in our attitudes if we submitted to the sovereignty of God and recognized that wherever we are, by our choosing or not, God's hand put us there. Imagine if we trusted so faithfully, like Mordecai, that God had a plan.

Are you where you hoped you would be at this point in your life? Do you have the children, the career, the body, or the house you wanted? Are your friends and relatives all you hoped they would be? Do you feel wanted and loved?

Esther's account reminds us that we aren't randomly placed in this chaotic world. God chose our family. He knows us inside and out. He has allowed some of the frustrations we have to be part of our lives.

Esther had to be persuaded to help her people. It would have been safest—and the least nerve wracking—to remain silent. But Mordecai reminded her and us that we are here, in the position we are in, for the works God has prepared for us to do.

She faced death. It's easy for us to fall into complacency and sit on the sidelines when we have much less to lose. As long as the persecution is on the other side of the world, we don't need to worry about it. As long as we're not the ones falling victim to natural disaster, we can quickly forget about those who are. We dismiss problems, because they are too big for one person, instead of being a part, even if it's a small part, of the solution.

It's easy to sit back and let others bear the brunt of kingdom work, too. Our sinful nature desires a selfish use of our time, talents, and treasures instead of graciously and generously giving to God and His work.

Someone else can teach Sunday school this year. Let someone else serve at the funeral or play the organ or lead a Bible study.

Oh, but how gracious God is when we step out in faith. Just as He was with Esther and worked through her to change the king's heart and save her people, God works through our small actions to do great things in the hearts and lives of others. Serving isn't a burden. It's a privilege to be counted worthy for God to use us.

The writer of Hebrews says, "God is not unjust; he will not forget your work and the love you have shown him as you have helped his people and continue to help them. We want each of you to show this same diligence to the very end, in order to make your hope sure. We do not want you to become lazy, but to imitate those who through faith and patience inherit what has been promised" (6:9–12).

And let's not forget the importance of Mordecai. He took Esther in after her parents died, and when she was taken to the king's harem, he waited for word of how she was doing, no doubt continually praying for her safety and protection. He informed her of the plot, because it would directly affect her, and he spurred her to get involved.

We need friends and/or family or church members to advise us, inform us, and spur us on, too. The writer of Hebrews said, "Let us hold unswervingly to the hope we profess, for he who promised is faithful. And let us consider how we may spur one another on toward love and good deeds" (10:23–24).

Not only do we need people to encourage us, but we need to encourage others to trust in God and His ways, even when we're unsure of the outcome. We can spur others to love, even when they are treated with hatred. We spur others to do good despite oppression and struggle.

Which battles are you being called to fight? How has God put you "in a position for such a time as this" to make a difference for Him? If you aren't sure, then pray God would show you and give you the strength to work for Him for His glory.

Devotion Question: No soldier would go to war without the proper equipment; nor would he purposely deny himself food or sleep when energy is required for the mission. What can you do physically and spiritually to face the battles you need to confront each day?

Topics for further study:

OVERCOMING OBSTACLES

1. Read John 16:33. Jesus doesn't sugarcoat anything. What is the problem with those who claim we can all live a happy, healthy, prosperous life if only we just believe?

2. Jesus said He overcame the world. He didn't say He would overcome all our troubles. My study Bible notes the difference between what we will have in Jesus and what we will have in the world.[10]

   In Jesus we have _____.

   In the world we have _____.

   How did Jesus overcome the world?

3. Read 1 Kings 16:29–33. What kind of man was Ahab?

4. Read 1 Kings 17:1–5. What kind of man was Elijah?

5. Read 1 Kings 17:6. How did Elijah survive the first part of the drought?

6. Read 1 Kings 18:1–10. What was Ahab doing during the three years of drought (v. 10)?

7. Read 1 Kings 18:16–18. What was Ahab's perception of what happened during the three years?

---

[10] *Concordia Self-Study Bible New International Version,* 1639.

8. Have you noticed that we, like Ahab, have a tendency to hate the consequences of sin without hating the sin? When my headstrong decisions and careless words cause divisions in my relationships, I despise the conflict that ensues and get frustrated when things fall apart. What are some of your pet sins, and what consequences do you find yourself frustrated about?

9. Think of Elijah's life during the three years of drought. What was he doing without?

10. Read 1 Kings 17:7–16. How did God take care of Elijah when he couldn't move about freely or enjoy the comforts of "home"?

11. God wants us to make sure we understand that we will face obstacles. Life in a fallen world guarantees as much, but God doesn't abandon us during those obstacles. He provides for us sometimes hour by hour. Can you think of times and ways God has helped you miraculously in difficult circumstances?

12. Can you think of people God put in your life to provide for you?

13. Read Judges 6:12–16. What task did God give Gideon?

14. Read Judges 7:1–8. What had been Gideon's original excuse as to why he wasn't the one to save Israel from Midian?

15. God cut the army of thirty-two thousand men to three hundred. Why (v. 2)?

16. Read Judges 7:19–25. How much fighting did the three hundred men do?

17. Sometimes the obstacles we face come from sources out of our control, but just as often the obstacle in front of us is from within. That obstacle may be called "pride," "fear," or "shame," but it's all a result of sin. How do we overcome ourselves so we can do the tasks God has in mind for us to do?

Sometimes God gives us the strength to overcome obstacles, and sometimes He provides other people to fight our battles. At other times God fights the battle for us. It's important is to put our trust in Him and not shy away from whatever He puts before us because He is with us.

BEING TEACHABLE WITH TOTAL OBEDIENCE

18. Read 1 Samuel 13:5-14. My study Bible notes that "Saul thought he could strengthen Israel's chance against the Philisthens while

disregarding the instruction of the Lord's prophet Samuel."[11] Why was it wrong for Saul to offer the sacrifice?

19. What did God think of Saul's disobedience?

20. Read 1 Samuel 15:1–3. Write down the words Samuel used in instructing Saul.

21. Read 1 Samuel 15:7–11. What did Saul do?

22. We're starting to see a pattern here. Saul was going to do things his way, not God's. Someone could argue that Saul was "trying" to do the right thing by offering the sacrifice and almost completing the mission God had given him. Yet God shows us He is after total obedience. It's easy to settle for good enough. What implication does this truth have for our lives?

23. Keep your page in 1 Samuel and flip to read Matthew 16:24–26. Look at the words Jesus used, words like *deny, follow, save, lose, find, gain, forfeit,* and *exchange.* Jesus told us we have choices that have earthly and eternal consequences. What does it mean to do things God's way?

24. What are the spiritual traits we're going to pursue to obey God?

---

[11] *Concordia Self-Study Bible New International Version,* 391.

25. Can you think of something you watched on TV that was offensive to God? Can you think of a behavior you've neglected to correct, one that dishonors God? What would total obedience have you do?

26. Read 1 Samuel 15:24–25. What was Saul's reason for not obeying the Lord completely?

27. That seems to clue us into another trait we must possess to be totally obedient to God. What is it?

28. Read Proverbs 9:8. If Saul had been teachable and interested in obeying the Lord, how would he have reacted in these two instances when Samuel confronted him?

29. Read 1 Samuel 20:24–33. When David didn't go to the New Moon Festival, Saul demanded that Jonathon account for David's absence. How did Saul respond when Jonathon said he'd allowed David to go home?

30. Why did Saul want David dead (v. 31)?

31. How did Saul respond when Jonathon stuck up for David (v. 33)?

32. Jonathon understood that God had given the kingdom to David, and Jonathon was okay with that. What traits would Saul need to be okay with God's plan for the kingdom?

33. We didn't read 1 Samuel 15:12, but if we had, we would have seen that Saul had gone to Carmel to set up a monument in his honor. Saul wanted to make and preserve a name for himself. His life shows what it looks like to be unteachable or feel you are above reproach. Total obedience requires that we (1) acknowledge our sin, not excuse or justify it, but learn from it; (2) be willing to do the right thing, even when it's unpopular; and (3) be humble enough to recognize and accept when God's plan is different from our own. Are you willing to apologize and accept responsibility for being wrong? Are you humble enough to do things another's way, or do you need to run the show? Are you willing to be persecuted for God's Word?

ADVICE

34. Read Daniel 6:1–9. Daniel was one of three administrators who answered to Darius. Why did Darius set administrators over the satraps (v. 2)?

35. What was the motive behind the satraps and administrators coming up with their plan (vv. 3-4)?

36. What kind of man was Daniel (v. 4)?

37. How was the plan of the satraps in direct opposition to the king's goals for the kingdom?

38. Darius listened to the plan of the administrators and satraps. How did the satraps deceive Darius (v. 7)?

39. Most of us can't imagine agreeing to a plan that would have people praying to us, but we aren't in a position of absolute power; nor are we of the pagan, polytheistic mind-set. What kinds of temptations might our friends give us in the form of advice?

40. Read Daniel 6:24. What was Darius's response when he realized the satraps' order was for their gain, not for the good of the kingdom?

41. We obviously aren't going to throw our friends into a lions' den. How should we respond to bad advice, even if it's from our Christian friends?

42. Read the following passages and write down the qualities you want in those you go to for advice.

Proverbs 13:20

Proverbs 15:33

Proverbs 16:13

43. Read Mark 8:31–33. What is another attribute we want in a friend we go to for advice?

Many years ago I wrote down a quote from Chuck Swindoll: "None are more formidable instruments of temptation than well-meaning friends who care more for our comfort than our character." A friend who wants us to be happy doesn't necessarily have the things of God in mind. As we saw when we looked at total obedience, often the way God wants and expects us to go is the path of denial to self and loss. A godly friend is going to advise you to take the path that honors God, even when it's the harder thing to do. Notice also that with both Darius and Jesus, they didn't seek advice. Others offered advice, even when it wasn't solicited. We must be careful when our friends offer us unsolicited advice, too. If the advice honors God, great. If it doesn't, we dare not take it. By the same token, we need to be careful about offering unsolicited advice to others. When we do offer advice, we need to make sure it's in line with God's Word.

SOMETHING TO THINK ABOUT

While we want to remain teachable to those in authority over us who know and understand the Word, we want to be closed off to the philosophies of the world, which can lead us astray. While we want godly friends to help and advise us, we want to be sure we're going to God for advice and direction. It seems that tact and gentleness are going to play a part, both in the Christian community and in the secular community, so we can stand our ground without being offensive. And yet at times the Word of God is offensive, even to those believers who are spiritually immature. How are you going to walk that tightrope, and what tools will you need?

Prayer to close the Lesson:

Good and gracious Father in heaven, thank You for putting us here right now, even if it isn't a place of our choosing. Forgive us for the messes our sinful lives create. Help us to be teachable, humble, selfless, and repentant of our sins. Give us the courage to obey You when it's the hard thing to do, even when facing persecution from those around us. Put people in our lives, such as Mordecai, who remind us that following and obeying You are the reason we are here. Let our actions glorify You now and always. In Jesus' name. Amen.

LESSON NINE

Martha

READ LUKE 10:38–42; JOHN 11:1–6, 17–43; 12:1–8.

Devotion: How hard it must have been for poor Martha. Haven't we all been there? She was tired, anxious, and stressed out; and there Mary sat while Martha worked. Finally, at the end of her rope, she went to Jesus. Surely He would defend her and tell Mary to get moving—only she, not Mary, was chastised.

What could be better than serving Jesus? If Martha had sat as Mary did, who would have made the food?

We know from other biblical accounts that Jesus didn't concern Himself about when or what He was going to eat. He fasted forty days before quoting Deuteronomy 8:3. "Man does not live on bread alone, but on every word that comes from the mouth of the Lord." When Jesus fed the five thousand, the thousands following Him had been with him three days and were out of food (Matt. 15:32). Jesus stayed and spoke to the Samaritan woman at the well while His disciples went to get food. When they returned and told Him to eat, He replied, "My food is to do the will of Him who sent me and to do His work. Do you not say 'Four months more and then the harvest?' I tell you, open your eyes and look at the fields! They are ripe for harvest" (John 4:34–35).

Jesus wanted Martha to put temporal things in their proper place and look at situations through an eternal perspective.

How often do we overlook that neighbor, friend, or coworker who needs to know his or her Savior, because we're so wrapped up in our own lives? We work hard to make things "perfect" for our families or friends for birthdays and holidays but forget to bring anything spiritual into the conversation. We complain about so much but forget to tell others about all God has done for us.

Jesus said to Martha, His disciples, and us, "Don't worry about food. Forget your stomach and your things and search for souls!"

When Lazarus fell ill, we see Jesus exhibiting the same perspective. Mary and Martha brought Lazarus's situation to Jesus, knowing He was their only hope. Jesus made them wait to give Him the opportunity to exhibit His power.

It wasn't for Mary and Martha's benefit that Lazarus had to die. Martha's faith didn't waver. Meeting Jesus, she said, "Lord, if you had been here, my brother would not have died. But I know that even now God will give you whatever you ask" (John 11:5). They needed only to be told of these things to believe them. His disciples, who were witnesses to these displays of Jesus' power, still doubted. Jesus said to them, "Lazarus is dead, and for your sake I am glad I was not there, so that you may believe."

Isn't that good for us to remember as we go through trials? It isn't always just for our refining that we go through trials, but sometimes it's for the benefit of others. It would be nice if God would always heal us miraculously, make financial or parenting problems disappear instantly, or give us the job of our dreams the first time we apply. If that were the case, would we readily credit God? Would we have access to others who need to hear about God and need the hope we have to get through their situation?

Often it is only after we've reached rock bottom that we're transparent with our lives and willing to share our trials with friends. It's only after we've been sustained that we feel the magnitude of God's provision as He supplies all we need to endure.

It's interesting to note, too, that when it came time to raise Lazarus, Martha told Jesus there would be an odor in the tomb. She'd just confessed that Jesus was the Messiah, and yet when He told the men to roll away the stone, she felt she must educate Him.

When we examine our prayer lives, we might find that we do the same. Isn't it easy to feel we need to tell God the truth of a situation, forgetting that He sees our hearts and weighs our motives? How easy it is to tell Him the best way to answer our prayers, too, as if He doesn't know.

With the account of Mary's anointing Jesus, we see the sisters again; their personalities are now clear. Martha was again serving. Mary is often talked about. She was dramatic and bold about her acts of worship. She fell at Jesus' feet after Lazarus died. She poured perfume on Jesus' feet. Mary showed her faith.

Martha's service, her act of worship, was less conspicuous but no less important. Once it was done with the right attitude, one that didn't compare her service to the service or lack of service of another (not begrudgingly but willingly), it both honored God and provided a useful service.

It may be that your work for God's kingdom is done outside the visible church, while others in the church receive glory and recognition for their efforts. Every act of service, when done with a pure heart and not "reluctantly or under compulsion" (2 Cor. 9:7), is valuable in God's eyes.

In fact, Jesus often operated undercover. Nicodemus came to Jesus to learn at night. Jesus stayed to talk to the Samaritan woman at the well while His disciples left for food. On several occasions, Jesus isolated Himself to pray. Some of His miracles were done in front of only Peter, James, and John. Other times when He healed someone, He asked the person not to tell others. He wasn't showy with His acts of service. In fact, if it weren't for the Holy Spirit, we wouldn't know about these things at all.

May God bless us as we serve Him in our own way. And may we glorify Him through our humble or dramatic acts of worship.

Devotion Question: At a recent Bible study, one of my friends mentioned she was a follower. "Give me something to do, and I'll do it," she said, "but I don't want to be in charge."

Sometimes we forget the blessing of the follower. Leaders are fantastic, but we need followers, too. A Sunday school superintendent needs Sunday school teachers. To put on events we need people willing to show up and help out. Are you a follower? If so, thank you for your help.

If you're a leader think of a few people you know who have come alongside you to help you out and send them a thank you and a token of your appreciation.

Topics for further study

BELIEVING, DOUBTING, DOING MIRACLES

1. Read Matthew 9:20–22, 27–29; and Luke 8:49–55.

What was the first thing the woman who quit bleeding, the blind men who received their sight, and Jairus did that resulted in healing?

2. Read James 1:5–8. What did James tell us to do if we lack wisdom (insight)?

3. What can we expect if we doubt God's ability or willingness to answer our prayers?

4. Read Hebrews 11:6. Is pleasing God something you set your heart to do? Does it make it on your list of goals? Maybe it's not something you consider. Shouldn't it be?

The writer of Hebrews tells us one thing we can do to please God. We can put our "firm belief in the honesty, reliability of another; confident expectation, hope[12]" in God. This pleases Him. Haven't we trusted a million less reliable things: the latest health craze, our crazy friends, our unstable relatives, a politician, newscaster, a famous sport personality? Why is it easy to put our hope and confidence in them and forget about the ultimate authority on everything? If we want to please God, we must start with the basics. We must start by putting our confidence, trust, and hope in Him.

5. The writer of Hebrews said that anyone who comes to God must do two things. What are they?

6. What does it mean to earnestly seek God?

7. Read Matthew 14:22–31. What did Jesus say immediately before Peter asked to come to Him?

8. Why did Peter begin to sink (v. 30)?

---

[12] Webster's New World Dictionary, 3rd College ed., s.v. "trust."

9. If we let it, fear will overtake courage. What stresses and distractions keep you from trusting God?

10. Read Mark 9:20–24. Make this your game plan for the days when you feel overwhelmed and when doubts arise and faith is running low. First, the man came to Jesus. When Jesus pointed out the man's lack of faith, the man didn't stomp off. He didn't argue about how great his faith really was. He professed belief and prayed for help to get over his lack of trust.

Do you have people in your life with whom you can be completely transparent, whom you can confide in when your faith is weak? These people can encourage you and pray for you when you lack strength.

11. Read Matthew 21:21-22. Should we expect miracles?

12. Read Romans 8:28 and 2 Corinthians 12:7–10. What if the miracle we expect doesn't happen?

13. Have you considered the role hardship may play in your life? Although we always want God to answer our prayers the way we think is best, sometimes God allows something in our lives we wouldn't want because it keeps us depending on Him. Arrogance or a false sense of security sometimes leads us to think we don't need God in our lives, but trouble usually sends us running back to God. If hardship keeps us close to God,

isn't it a blessing and not a hardship? What hardship are you enduring, and how does it affect you spiritually?

14. Something else to consider is how our choices put us on a road we don't want to be on. If we smoke for twenty years, we may end up with emphysema. An unhealthy diet or years of too little sleep may lead to our demise. Should we expect God to miraculously save us from our unhealthy choices? Why or why not?

15. Read Hebrews 5:7–10. Picture Jesus praying in the garden of Gethsemane. This is one time when Jesus' prayers were recorded for us. What was Jesus' emotional state?

16. Did Jesus get what He asked for?

17. Although God the Father could have saved Jesus from death, He chose to allow Jesus to suffer. What did Jesus learn through His suffering (v. 8)?

18. It's easy to obey when we're asked to do what we want to do. It can be quite a bit harder when we're asked to do what we don't want to do. What did this obedience produce in Jesus (v. 9)?

A missionary friend of mine pointed out that in the New Testament, this word, perfection, often refers to someone or something that arrives at its intended goal or fulfills its purpose. Jesus was already sinless, but His suffering made Him perfect. A note in my study Bible explains, "Christ had not been morally or spiritually imperfect, but his incarnation was completed (perfected) when he experienced suffering. He identified with us on the deepest level of anguish, and so became qualified to pay the price for our sinful imperfection and to become our sympathetic high priest."[13]

19. Sometimes God tells us no to refine and perfect us. What attributes does suffering produce in us?

20. Why is it important that we attain these attributes? What purpose may they achieve?

In the process of editing this book, two flash drives met their demise. Twice I had to retype all or portions of studies. The first time I took the trials in stride. When the same thing happened two weeks later, I made some long-overdue changes. I was using flash drives because I was working more and more on my laptop. The family computer was hard to work on because certain keys on the keyboard had been sticking for some time. My writing computer was uncomfortable for typing and was outdated.

School was back in session, and my high-school-age daughter was going to need to do lots of typing for her classes. Losing my work made replacing that keyboard a priority, and as I talked the

[13] *Concordia Self-Study Bible New International Version*, 1878.

matter over with my husband, we decided that, considering how slow the computer was, replacing it was an even better option.

God used my dead flash drives as a means to wake me up to something that should have gotten my attention sooner. I wonder whether my daughter, who'd already struggled through typing one paper, hadn't prayed that we'd replace that keyboard.

Imagine if God is using the adversity in your life to answer the prayer of another. My prayer now is that God might open my eyes to things I need to do without the adversity. Unfortunately I'm dull, and often it is only through pain that I get the hint. Sometimes we need to remember to thank the Lord for the pain.

THE ATTITUDE OF THE HEART

21. Read Hosea 7:14–16. What do we often do when something isn't going well for us (v. 14)?

22. Does that work?

23. What is God looking for (vv. 14, 16)?

24. Does that mean there is no place for tears?

25. What changed in Martha between the first time we read of her and the last? In both scenarios she served Jesus.

Read the following verses and write down what the passage teaches us about what our attitude should be.

Ephesians 4:22–5:2

26. Put off your_____because it is _____ and _____ (4:22).

27. Put on your _____ which is_____and_____(4:24).

28. How do we take off our old self and put on our new self? What does that task entail?

29. Speak the _____ (4:25).

30. Do you tell people what they want to hear, or do you speak the truth?

31. Don't sin in your _____ or hold onto your _____ (4:26).

32. Don't give the Devil a _____
    (4:27). In other words, don't make things easy for him.

33. Do you find yourself remembering hateful things people have
    done to you?

34. Don't _____, but instead do something
    _____ (4:28).

35. Stealing is taking something that doesn't belong to you, and it is
    wrong, regardless of the value. If you take your coworker's can
    of soda or cookie without his or her knowledge or approval, you
    have just stolen something. What other seemingly small things
    are easy to swipe?

36. Use your mouth to _____, not
    for _____ (4:29).

Using our mouths in this way is hard on so many levels. First, it
requires self-control, and that requires prayer. Ask yourself whether
something is necessary and nice before letting something leave
your lips. If the answer is no to either, refrain or rephrase.

37. The Holy Spirit is your comforter and counselor. Don't
    _____ Him by making things hard for Him or
    being resistant to learning (4:30).

38. Get rid of all _____ ,

_____,

_____,

_____,

_____,

_____ (4:31).

Here are the definitions of these words:

Bitterness is being "resentful; cynical".[14]

Rage is "furious, uncontrolled anger".[15]

Anger is "hostile feelings because of opposition, a hurt".[16]

Brawling is "to quarrel or fight noisily".[17]

Slander is "the utterance of a falsehood that damages another's reputation".[18]

(If it doesn't need to be said, don't say it!)

Malice is the "desire to harm another; evil intent".[19] This is a sin. We may very well know we're not going to set someone's hair on fire, but we spend an afternoon daydreaming about doing so anyway. What cruel thoughts have you entertained lately?

---

[14] Webster's New World Dictionary, 3rd College ed., s.v. "bitter."

[15] Webster's New World Dictionary, 3rd College ed., s.v. "rage."

[16] Webster's New World Dictionary, 3rd College ed., s.v. "anger."

[17] Webster's New World Dictionary, 3rd College ed., s.v. "brawl."

[18] Webster's New World Dictionary, 3rd College ed., s.v. "slander."

[19] Webster's New World Dictionary, 3rd College ed., s.v. "malice."

39. Be _____ and
_____ and
_____ like Christ (4:32).

Jesus was able to overlook the cruel behavior of those who tortured Him. What are you unable to overlook that compares to that? Probably not much.

40. First Peter 4:1–2 tells us to be done with _____. That means don't excuse, justify, or relish it. Be done with it.

41. When you are done with something, how is your attitude affected?

Notice that Peter told us to arm ourselves with the attitude that Christ had, namely to be willing to suffer, knowing there was a bigger purpose. Often we fight every battle and correct every wrong only to lose a relationship. Jesus didn't do that. If He had, all Scripture would describe Him constantly pointing out sin.

42. First Peter 4:7–11 reminds us that the end of all things is near. We don't know whether we'll live another day, and none of us knows when judgment day is near. How does that affect our attitude?

43. This passage tells us our love shouldn't be superficial but deep. What differences will there be in our lives when our love is deep?

44. What is the "attitude adjustment" check in verse 9?

45. Finally, Peter reminded us that our time, talents, and treasures were given to us for what purpose?

46. I love the statement in verse 11. If anyone serves (using his or her spiritual gifts), he or she should do so with the strength God provides. What's the difference between our strength and God's?

SOMETHING TO THINK ABOUT

When is the last time you approached the work of the Lord or anything spiritual with urgency? Have you prayed for people with urgency realizing your prayers can make a difference in someone's eternal life? Often the only thing that receives urgency in our lives is getting somewhere or reaching the TV on time. What will it take to shift your urgency from earthly things to heavenly things?

Prayer to Close the Lesson:

Heavenly Father, forgive us for weeping and complaining about life instead of turning to You. Forgive us for thoughtless words or hymns uttered when our minds were far from You. Forgive us for grumbling while serving You. Thank You, Jesus, for suffering for me. Thank You for going through all You did so You can relate to my pain, sorrow, worry, and fear. Holy Spirit, forgive me for stubbornly refusing to change and for ignoring Your prompting. Teach my heart and mind to respond to You. To You—Father, Son, and Holy Spirit—be endless glory and praise. Amen.

LESSON TEN

Mary

READ LUKE 10:38–42; JOHN 12:1–3.

Devotion: Oh, to be like Mary with a heart and mind devoted to her Lord! How many of us intend to spend time reading the Word and praying every day, but the days come and go, and there is cleaning to do, errands or a garden to tend, and so many other things beckon? Mary didn't care what got done. Her Lord was there, and she couldn't imagine being anywhere but in His presence.

If we leave praying and reading the Word for when they fit in our schedule, our sinful nature will remind us of a million seemingly important things to do until every second of our day is spent. We wouldn't dream of missing a favorite TV show, time with a best friend, or a phone call from a loved one, and yet we readily put time with God on the back burner, or we give Him just a few minutes.

The first commandment tells us to fear (stand in awe), love, and trust in God above all things. The demonic army is good at tempting us to break this. If only they could keep us "busy." If only they could convince us we know enough, and our prayers don't matter anyway.

James reminded us, "The prayer of a righteous man is powerful and effective. Elijah was a man just like us. He prayed earnestly that it would not rain, and it did not rain on the land for three and a half years. Again he prayed and the heavens gave rain, and the earth produced its crops" (James 5:16–18).

Our fellow Christians need our prayers. Those who are ill and imprisoned need prayers for healing and strength. Prayers on behalf of our country may change the way our rulers lead. Proverbs 21:1 says, "The king's heart is in the hand of the Lord. He directs it like a watercourse wherever He pleases." God invites us to pray and hears us when we do. Perhaps it's the most tangible way we can change the world. I can't destroy a terror cell, but I can pray that God would destroy those factions of evil that persecute believers. I can't free the Christians in labor camps, but I can pray for God to move on their behalf, to strengthen and support them, and to provide for them. I can pray that He would sustain their faith, so even if they die a martyr's death, they will receive the reward of a believer.

James said, "You do not have, because you do not ask God" (4:2). Dear friends, let that not be true of us. God will answer our prayers according to His perfect will, but let's not allow evil to prevail on our watch.

Mary not only made time for Jesus, but she demonstrated her love for Him without hesitation or embarrassment. She poured perfume on Jesus' feet in front of His disciples. She didn't care who saw or knew. Jesus had raised her brother from the dead, and she would worship Him without restraint.

How hard this is to do, even among believers. For years several of us in my church talked about kneeling to pray after Communion. We wanted to show our reverence to God in this way after receiving such a great gift. We had the freedom to pray however we wanted. So what kept us from doing so? Mostly we just lacked the courage.

It was only after studying Mary that I decided to kneel. She professed her admiration boldly and faced opposition; I could kneel without worry of adversity. What was my excuse?

Do we show unabashed devotion in our conversations and church attendance, with a silent prayer before eating a meal at work or in public?

Jesus said, "Whoever acknowledges me before men, I will acknowledge before my Father in heaven" (Matt. 10:32; Luke 12:8).

Peter denied His Lord and found forgiveness. We find that same forgiveness when we repent of the times we've shrunk from opportunities to show others our admiration for Christ. Once he was forgiven, Peter changed. On Pentecost he was the one boldly proclaiming who Christ was and what He'd done.

We didn't read of it, but Mary was criticized for her lavish display of worship. Like Mary, we need to be prepared to face persecution from people who don't share our love of Jesus. We can find comfort in knowing that God sees our devotion to Him, and this will be rewarded in eternity.

Devotion Question: The Pharisees were known for being showy with their acts of righteousness while not having true devotion to God. What is the difference between putting on a religious show and unabashedly showing your devotion to God without worry of embarrassment?

Topics for further study:

WORSHIP

1. Read Matthew 2:1–2. Why did the wise men embark on their journey?

2. Read Matthew 2:9–12. What did the magi feel when they saw the house where the star had come to rest?

3. How did the magi worship Jesus?

4. What did they show by bowing to Jesus, a small child?

God revealed Himself and His Son to these wise men. Once He did, these men embarked on a journey that may have taken some time to complete. My study Bible says, "Tradition has them coming from Arabia or Persia."[20]

---

[20] *Concordia Self-Study Bible New International Version*, 1449.

I've also heard that perhaps they were the result of Daniel's time in Babylon when he was chief of the wise men and magicians. Perhaps the lessons and prophecies he knew were handed down for generations.

At any rate, the wise men left their homeland and busy lives to seek Jesus, not hoping to "get" anything from Him but merely to bow before Him, pay Him honor, and present Him with their gifts. When they found the house, they were filled with abundant joy. Then, after they had been warned not to go back to Herod, a worldly king of power and prestige, they obeyed and took an alternate route.

This seems to be a good example for us concerning worship. Seek God in reverence, joyfully worship Him, present Him with our thank offerings, listen to the Word of God, and obey it.

5. Read John 4:21–24. What things are irrelevant when it comes to worship?

6. What is God looking for when we worship Him?

7. Jesus said it was important to worship in truth. What truths do we need to profess in order to worship God as we should?

8. Place is not an issue, but truth is. What implications does this have in terms of the worship services offered at church and elsewhere?

9. Read 1 Corinthians 14:26–33. Imagine that you arrived at church and the pastor went to the front of the church, asking what hymn should be sung to begin worship. There may be as many different responses as people in attendance. Someone might respond, "We did that hymn last week!" Someone else might mutter, "I hate that melody!" under his or her breath. What's the problem with conducting "worship" this way?

DISTRACTION

10. Read Matthew 22:1–14. Read verse 5 again. Why didn't the people come to the banquet?

11. How can our house, lawn, garage, and possessions keep us from Bible study, prayer, or service in God's kingdom?

12. What other things can keep you from Bible study, prayer and service to God?

13. What practical steps can you take to make sure that doesn't happen?

Some of my friends start the day with Bible study and prayer to ensure they don't get overlooked in the busyness of the day. I prefer to do mine in the evening after my kids go to bed. That means I need to make sure to get to it before I become too tired to comprehend what I'm doing.

I heard a woman on a radio program talk about how she made the decision to get up an hour earlier each day to pray and read her Bible. She was astounded at the difference the change made in her life as she saw prayers answered, prayers she previously hadn't taken the time to pray.

Isn't it sad to think of the things in your life that might be different if you took the time to pray about them? James wrote, "You do not have because you do not ask" (4:2).

Isn't it equally sad to think of the relationship you could have with your heavenly Father but might not have because you don't take the time to be in the Word?

14. Read Luke 9:57–62. For the fox a hole is his home. The nest is a bird's home. Think of what is required to maintain a house. Certainly time is involved. What does a house require other than time and what temptations come with having a house?

15. A house can be a distraction, but it can also be a blessing. How so?

16. Concerning the man who wanted to bury his father, the note in my study Bible says, "If his father had already died, the man would have been occupied with the burial then. But evidently

he wanted to wait until after his father's death, which might have been years away. Jesus told him that the spiritually dead could bury the physically dead, and that the spiritually alive should be busy proclaiming the kingdom of God."[21]

The man said to Jesus, "I'll stay with my family until my father is dead, and then I won't have anything holding me back." What's the problem with that thinking?

17. Jesus left us with an image of a man holding a plow but looking back. Why would looking back be a problem?

If our house is an idol (something we put in the place of serving God) and we put all our time, energy, and money into it, we may never have time, energy, or money to use toward service to the kingdom. If we wait for the perfect time to serve God, it will never happen. If we do our part in the kingdom but constantly look over our shoulder at all we're giving up, Jesus said we aren't fit to serve Him. He's looking for total commitment. He's looking for us to get rid of the things that keep us from kingdom work. Are you ready to give something up to serve Him more? If so, what will that be?

---

[21] *Concordia Self-Study Bible New International Version*, 1568.

18. Read Matthew 6:19–21. How will we keep our house, life, or thirst for entertainment from becoming a distraction that keeps us from more important things?

19. Time seems to be a factor. Not only do we easily fill our time, but we forget to go about the work of God with urgency. Why is that important?

20. Read Matthew 13:3–9, 22. What sort of things distract the person who represents the seed sown among weeds?

21. Have you ever wasted a day, night, or week in worry or despair over a situation? What is wrong with that?

22. Read 1 Corinthians 15:58. How much of ourselves should we give to the work of the Lord?

23. Does that mean we shouldn't take care of our houses, an aging parent, or children? How do we know?

God doesn't want anything in our lives to become an idol. If we do what we're doing for earthly glory, we do so for the wrong reasons, and we excuse ourselves from working in the kingdom. It may be a legitimate step to back out of ministry to spend more time with our families, to care for an aging parent, or to go to work to get money for our family. It's all about motive.

God expects us to take care of our families, but we shouldn't use our families, housework, or anything else as an excuse not to help. We're all busy.

When we do work for the Lord, we should do it wholeheartedly. We don't want to be the person with the plow who looks over his or her shoulder at all he or she is missing. We want to look straight ahead, hands on the plow and working with all our hearts.

JOY

24. There are 218 references to *joy* in the Bible, 236 if you add *joyous* and *joyful*. My dictionary said *joy* is "a very glad feeling; happiness; delight[22]." How does spiritual joy differ from happiness?

25. Galatians 5:22 tells us joy is evidence of what?

26. Read Galatians 5:16–21. How do we produce the fruit of the Spirit?

To emphasize: By not _____ (16)
the desires of the _____ (16)
nature because the sinful nature _____(17)
what is _____ (17) to the Spirit.
Instead, be_____ (18) by the Spirit.

---

[22] Webster's New World Dictionary, 3rd College ed., s.v. "joy."

27. The sinful nature is our natural state. Joy isn't natural for us. Paul gives us some characteristics of the sinful nature in verses 19–21. Which of those characteristics stand in the way of being joyful?

28. Read James 1:2–4. What does James say ought to bring us joy?

29. I don't know about you, but joy isn't the first thing that comes to mind when I'm in the midst of trying times. James tells us trials test our faith. How so?

When James talked about perseverance, I think of exercising. Maybe you've had an episode in your life when you took a break from exercising and eating healthy foods, gained some weight, and later rededicated yourself to exercise and a healthy lifestyle. The first days of exercise don't take you instantly back to a fit body. In fact, the first weeks of working out typically result in weight gain and little to no noticeable difference in your body, except maybe the adverse effects of aches and pains. But if you continue, you will notice subtle differences; calf and bicep muscles are more defined; pants aren't so tight around the waist.

Persevering spiritually does the same thing. Trials test our faith. Do we really believe God is bigger than this situation? Are we confident of God's love in the midst of the mess? When we go back to the Word for confidence of His promises, we build spiritual muscles. We chip away at worry and doubt, and we replace them with rock-solid faith, a mature faith, that not only sustains us but is healthy enough so we can teach and encourage others during their trials, too.

30. How can the strengthening of our faith muscles result in joy?

31. Read Matthew 28:8. What two things were the women feeling?

32. How does that comfort us?

33. Can you think of a time in your life when you were joyful but also felt another emotion?

34. Read John 15:5–11. Jesus compared remaining in Him, living with love, and producing the fruits of faith to a branch staying connected to the vine. He followed this illustration by telling us the end product would be complete joy. Why is it so important that we get our joy in Christ?

35. *Complete* means "whole; entire"[23]. That means nothing is missing. Is that how you would describe the joy in your life?

36. If not, what might be the cause?

---

[23] Webster's New World Dictionary, 3rd College ed., s.v. "complete."

Something to Think About

I'm currently working a few days a week as an elderly companion to a retired pastor. The pastor is unable to communicate most of the time. Often when he is asked a question, he responds with a smile. He does the same to greet someone. When I come into the room, he isn't always able to say, "Good morning!" but he says as much with a smile.

Working with him has taught me the importance of living joyfully. He has won his caretakers over without saying a word, and he's able to witness his faith, even in the midst of a living situation most of us wouldn't choose.

He's taught me to speak less and smile more. Running around and looking stressed and frazzled hardly makes people want the life we have. That doesn't mean we should put on a fake smile that portrays a perfect life in the midst of struggle. As we make our time with God the priority it should be, He directs us and reminds us of what is important. He answers our prayers exponentially better than we are able, even when He says no to what we ask.

Think about that. Can you remember a time when the outcome wasn't what you wanted but God worked mightily in your life anyway?

Prayer to Close the Lesson:

Holy Father, You are worthy of our admiration and praise. You are also worthy of our time. Let our hearts be devoted to You. As we turn to You, fill us with abundant joy, knowing You are in control. Help us to see past the distractions in our lives so we can better serve You. In Jesus' name. Amen.

Lesson Eleven

Tabitha

READ ACTS 9:36-42.

Devotion: I like to take note of descriptions of people in the Bible. For instance, "Moses was a very humble man, more humble than anyone else on the face of the earth" (Numbers 12:3). Concerning Job, God said, "There is no one on earth like him; he is blameless and upright, a man who fears God and shuns evil" (Job 1:8). When King Darius called to Daniel in the lions' den, he addressed him as Daniel, "servant of the living God" (Dan. 6:20). Jesus said John the Baptist was a "lamp that burned and gave light" (John 5:35). Acts 9 refers to Tabitha as a disciple "who was always doing good and helping the poor." That is the essence of compassion. Compassion is "deep sympathy, pity."[24]

You cannot be compassionate when you are engrossed in your own life, because you won't notice another person's misfortune; and even if you do, you'll be too wrapped up in your own troubles

_____

[24] Webster's New World Dictionary, 3rd College ed., s.v. "compassion."

to care. To be compassionate, we must look beyond ourselves and notice the people around us. Would you notice if someone wasn't in church for a week or two? Do you notice when others are having a bad day? Do you notice if something is wrong at your neighbor's house?

A couple of years ago at a Bible study, a woman admitted that she didn't know her neighbors. In fact, the only names in the neighborhood she knew were the dogs' names, because she heard them being called so often. If you don't know your neighbor's names and haven't taken the time to get to know them, there is a good chance that they won't come to you when they're having problems.

How many times in any given day do you come in contact with people who need your help? Sometimes their needs are physical—help with getting their coat on, finding a ride, tying a shoe, or obtaining a meal. Sometimes the need is emotional: a word of encouragement, a smile, or a hug. Sometimes the need is spiritual: a verse of Scripture that speaks to the person's situation or a prayer uttered on his or her behalf.

Tabitha made clothes to give to the widows and the poor. She could have used her talents to earn money elsewhere. Instead of seeking worldly wealth with her talents, she used her talents to benefit others instead of herself.

Jesus said in Luke 12:29 and following,

> Do not set your heart on what you will eat or
> drink; do not worry about it. For the pagan world

runs after all such things, and your Father knows that you need them. But seek his kingdom, and these things will be given to you as well. Do not be afraid, little flock, for your Father has been pleased to give you the kingdom. Sell your possessions and give to the poor. Provide purses for yourselves that will not wear out, a treasure in heaven that will not be exhausted, where no thief comes near and no moth destroys. For where your treasure is, there your heart will be also.

We can work for earthly treasure, or we can work for the Lord. That's not to say that you can't have a job and do God's work. Sometimes working allows us to do God's work. The apostle Paul made tents so he could travel and establish churches.

There's a distinction between using all our worldly income for ourselves and every moment outside of work for our own fulfillment, entertainment, hobbies, and so forth, and using our income, time, and talents as a means of furthering God's kingdom.

If we're going to be compassionate, maybe the first step is to be content. The apostle Paul said, "But godliness with contentment is great gain. For we brought nothing into the world, and we can take nothing out of it. But if we have food and clothing, we will be content with that. People who want to get rich fall into temptation and a trap and into many foolish and harmful desires that plunge men into ruin and destruction. For the love of money is a root of all kinds of evil. Some people, eager for money, have wandered from the faith and pierced themselves with many griefs" (1 Tim. 6:6–10).

If we aren't content, then we won't think we have anything to give. We'll still be building *our* earthly kingdom. We'll always have something more on the "I need" list. In our minds we'll justify not giving to others because we still don't have enough.

Don't we all have a home or shelter of some kind? Don't most of us have ten times the amount of clothes we need? Who of us has less than a week's worth of food in his or her home? That says nothing of our vehicles, toys, retirement and saving accounts. We're rich beyond measure. How could we not be content? How could we not look beyond ourselves?

Stepping outside of complacency to notice others doesn't need to be earth shattering. Pray that God would help you to see those who would benefit from your help, even in the smallest of ways. A card or phone call, a twenty-minute visit, or a five-dollar bouquet of flowers can mean a lot to someone.

Devotion Question: What hinders you from being compassionate? Many of us want to be compassionate, but things get in the way. Make a list of things that keep you from being compassionate and use it during your prayers in the coming days and weeks.

Topics for further study:

TO WHOM SHOULD WE BE COMPASSIONATE?

1. Read Galatians 6:10. When should we be compassionate?

2. To whom should we show compassion?

3. Read Luke 6:30. To whom should we give?

4. Does that mean we should never say no? In what circumstances would it be okay not to give to a person or organization?

When I did this Bible study with a group of ladies, we had quite a discussion concerning people who ask for money on street corners. Our local newspaper did a story in which the journalist followed a "homeless" person seeking money after he or she left the corner. The journalist found that the person had a car and an apartment. The journalist also followed the person into a store, where the person bought alcohol and cigarettes.

Some in our group said that was reason enough not to give to the person. We don't want to support someone else's addictions, and the Bible clearly tells us to work for our food. A capable person who begs for money is a form of corruption.

When I led a seminar several years ago now, this topic came up. A woman mentioned that she puts together a packet consisting of a granola bar, a bottle of water, and a Bible passage. She kept several packets in her car at all times, so she was always prepared to give something to anyone. Not only did she supply something for someone physically; she planted a seed spiritually, too.

What do you think?

5. Read Luke 10:25–37. List some reasons why the priest and Levite may not have stopped to help the man.

6. In what ways did the Samaritan show compassion to the man?

7. Jesus told this parable to teach us about compassion. Jesus didn't use the term *neighbor* to talk about someone who lives next to us. He used the term to show how we should treat others. To answer the teacher's question, who are we to treat like a neighbor?

8. If we're honest, we might not want to treat everyone as we treat our neighbor. Sometimes we're not very Christ-like to the people who live next to us. In fact, they might be shocked to hear we are Christians, or they may turn away from Christianity because we are the only image of Christ they've seen. How are we sometimes a poor neighbor to those who live near us?

9. Read 1 Timothy 5:8, 16. Sometimes we get so busy looking outward for people to help that we forget about the people right in front of us. Where are our time, energy, compassion, and heart of servitude to be used first?

10. We can lose sight of this truth on both ends of the spectrum. How do we maintain a balance of looking outward and inward?

11. How does the idea of "seasons of life" play into this balance?

12. Read Acts 20:33–35. Why did Paul make tents?

13. Much like Tabitha, Paul looked at work as a vehicle to show compassion. Because of his abilities, he was able to support others in the ministry and show compassion to those less fortunate. What abilities do you have that you could use to support those in ministry and show compassion to those around you?

Ways We Can Show Compassion

14. Read Ephesians 6:18–19. What is one task we can always do for others?

15. Notice verse 18. Paul tells us to be _____ and always to pray for the saints. What does that mean?

16. How can we pray for those in ministry?

17. Read 2 Kings 4:8–10. What did the woman from Shunem do for Elisha?

18. What do we know about the woman from Shunem?

19. Read 1 Kings 17:7–16. What did the woman do for Elijah?

20. What do we know about this woman?

21. What word is used in verse 9 to describe how God encouraged the woman to help?

22. The Shunammite woman was well-to-do and gave willingly out of her generosity. For the Sidonian widow, giving wasn't an option because she had nothing to give, yet God commanded her to be generous and provide what she needed so she could be generous. If you are honest in comparing the circumstances of your life to the Shunammite woman or the Sidonian widow, who are you most like? What do you have that you could give

to benefit God's kingdom? Is it a skill, time, money, or some other physical item?

23. We aren't told whether Tabitha was well-to-do or had a modest income. We don't know whether she had a husband or children. What we do know is that she gave her time, she used her talent, and she gave it to benefit those in need. She noticed the people around her. We aren't told that the woman of Shunem housed many people. We are told that she housed Elijah. The widow also took one person in. Sometimes we think that if we can't do a lot, we have nothing to give or won't make an impact. These accounts challenge that notion. Giving one pair of gloves to a child who has none makes a difference to that child. Giving rides to an elderly neighbor who has a clinic appointment or picking up groceries for a sick mom makes all the difference to that one person. Think of one person in your sphere of influence. What difference could you make in his or her life?

24. Read 1 Samuel 1:12–18. Eli wasn't the most compassionate person right off the bat. He made wrong assumptions that all but kicked a woman when she was down. Once Eli realized Hannah wasn't drunk but in anguish, what did he do?

25. Did he know what she wanted or why she was in anguish?

26. What can this story teach us?

27. Read Hebrews 3:13. What are we told to do?

28. How often?

29. Why?

Think of that. God tells us through the writer of Hebrews that we need to encourage each other every day because sin (pride, lies, anxiety, and so forth) can harden us. If we become hard, we are prone to bitterness. Paul told us in Ephesians 4:31 to "get rid of all bitterness, rage and anger, brawling and slander, along with every form of malice." In the next verse, he told us to "be kind and compassionate to one another, forgiving each other, just as in Christ God forgave you." Encouraging others may result in their being more compassionate and forgiving, and this step requires no money. What may it require?

SELFISHNESS AND GREED

30. Read Luke 12:13–21. What was the sin of the rich man?

31. Notice that a man came to Jesus, looking for a decision regarding his inheritance; Jesus instead told a parable about greed. This is a good lesson for us. Sometimes we get caught up in the politics of situations and miss the spiritual issue altogether. How can we keep from becoming overly invested in emotions so our focus is solely on what's temporal instead of what's eternal?

32. Read the following passages and write down the perspective from the passage that should help keep us from greed and selfishness with our possessions.

   Job 1:21

   Psalm 24:1

   Matthew 6:19–21

   Philippians 2:3–8

33. Read Colossians 3:5. Paul tells us that greed is really just a form of what?

34. Think of some ways our society excuses selfishness and greed.

I have found that often when I feel sorry for myself, this is because I'm focusing only on myself and not on others. When I look at the struggles of others and offer to walk beside them, I realize how good God has been to all of us and how painful life can sometimes be. Helping out a friend rarely just helps him or her. It helps our perspective, and we are blessed, too.

SOMETHING TO THINK ABOUT:

Our identity can't be based on our looks, accomplishments, or possessions, because any number of things (a car accident, diagnosis, or storm) could leave us without any of those things. Our identity must be based on being a child of God, and our value is that He cares for us so much that He chose to redeem us. We are precious in His sight.

Jesus had a knack for giving value to those who usually weren't on people's radar: the woman at the well, the lepers, the woman caught in adultery, the man who was demon possessed.

It's important that we start noticing the wallflowers, the lonely, the hurting, and those trapped in sin to let them know they are valuable in God's eyes. Pray that God would open your eyes to the people around you whom you might not notice. Find ways, even small ones, to lift them up and show compassion.

Prayer to Close the Lesson:

Heavenly Father, You have lavished us with earthly belongings and spiritual blessings. May we see the people You have put in our lives to help. Give us a generous spirit. Let our lives reflect Your goodness. Forgive us for so often concentrating only on ourselves. In Jesus' name we pray. Amen.

Made in the USA
Monee, IL
30 September 2019